THE UNIVERSITY OF MICHIGAN
CENTER FOR JAPANESE STUDIES

MICHIGAN PAPERS IN JAPANESE STUDIES
NO. 4

SURVEY OF JAPANESE COLLECTIONS
IN THE UNITED STATES

by

Naomi Fukuda

Ann Arbor

Center for Japanese Studies
The University of Michigan

1980

Funded by the Japan-United States Friendship Commission

ISBN 0-939512-09-2

Copyright © 1981

by

Center for Japanese Studies
The University of Michigan

Printed in the United States of America

TABLE OF CONTENTS

Preface	vii
Foreword, by Duane E. Webster	ix
Introduction	1

1. Profiles of Libraries

University of Arizona	6
University of California at Berkeley	9
Joint Project of UC Berkeley and Hoover Institution	17
University of California at Los Angeles	18
University of California at Santa Barbara	23
University of Chicago	26
Columbia University	31
Cornell University	37
Harvard University	42
University of Hawaii	48
Hoover Institution	54
University of Illinois	59
Indiana University	62
University of Kansas	65
Library of Congress	71
University of Maryland	94
University of Michigan	99
University of Minnesota	105
Ohio State University	109
University of Oregon	113
University of Pennsylvania	117
University of Pittsburgh	120
Princeton University	124
University of Rochester	128
University of Texas	131
University of Washington, Seattle	135
Washington University, St. Louis	142
University of Wisconsin	146
Yale University	150

TABLE OF CONTENTS, continued

2. Observations and Issues   157

    General Summary   158
    Categories of Libraries   159
    Collection Management   161
    Position in the University Library System   165

Appendices: Statistical Tables   167

    1. Resources of Libraries Surveyed   168
    2. Annual Growth of Collections   171
    3. Funding   172
    4. Geographical Distribution   173
    5. General Status of Collections   175
    6. Surveyed Libraries' Coverage
        of Selected Topics   180

Preface

Scholarly inquiry into any distant culture is considerably promoted when the materials on which it is based are made proximate to the inquiring scholar. The library, for a student of foreign things, is normally a sine qua non; for the work of U.S. scholars and students in Japanese studies, the collections surveyed here are a fundamental resource. Universities and centers sponsoring Japanese studies ought therefore to pay special attention to improving and maintaining them, and this publication represents part of the University of Michigan Center for Japanese Studies' effort toward that end.

Two recent surveys of note have considered academic programs on Japan at U.S. colleges and universities. The first, under the auspices of SSRC-ACLS, was published in 1970; the second, prepared for the Subcommittee on Japanese Studies of the American Panel of CULCON, was published in 1977. Neither was directed particularly at the library collections supporting the programs, although both pointed to the importance of such holdings. After a workshop which it sponsored for Japanese collection librarians August 28-30, 1978, in Washington, D.C., the Japan-United States Friendship Commission was moved to assist an in-depth survey of the particular and general state of the research collections in this country.

This volume contains the report of that survey, which provides librarians and others concerned with collection and service development with the kind of comparative data that is usually a spur to ambition. But the surveyors, sponsors, and others involved in the completion of this work are convinced that future development of these valuable collections depends on cooperation in services and coordination of acquisitions among them. To see themselves here gathered between two covers is in itself an achievement promising well for future cooperation.

> Robert E. Cole
> Director
> Center for Japanese Studies
> The University of Michigan

Foreword

A current concern of research library managers is securing more and better information on the development and uses of its collections. This information is needed for making critical decisions relating to distribution of limited resources, building or renovating facilities, introducing automated systems or simply maintaining current levels of effort during a period of intense fiscal pressures.

This interest in improved management information is particularly important to librarians committed to advancing the usefulness of Japanese collections in research universities. These collections support instructional and research programs within the university that are not richly funded or politically influential. Frequently, enrollments in Japanese studies are modest and research endeavors are limited.

The apparent popularity of other area studies and the push for career preparation in higher education have not benefitted Japanese studies. At the same time, the problems of maintaining Japanese collections are growing more acute. The wealth of Japanese intellectual and cultural output is expanding well beyond the capacity of research universities to handle it. The difficulties of bibliographic control both within Japan and here in the United States continue to harass the librarian as well as the user. The problems in learning what items are available and then securing these materials make the acquisition process expensive and labor intensive. And the lack of qualified and interested personnel to staff the Japanese collections and their libraries makes improved performance doubly difficult.

In the face of what appears to be a critical and sometimes hostile environment, the problems that face Japanese curators are evident. A workshop for Japanese/U.S. bibliographers coordinated by the Association of Research Libraries Office of Management Studies identified many of them in 1978.* The task now becomes to build an effective response to these pressures. The traditional response of securing more money for development of isolated collections as a way of resolving these concerns is most likely a limited possibility in the future. The greater potential lies with the applica-

---

* Association of Research Libraries, Office of Management Studies. <u>Workshop for Japanese Collection Librarians in American Research Libraries</u>: Washington, D.C., Author, 1978.

tion of technology, the extension of interinstitutional cooperation and the strengthening of the internal management of these collections.

The enclosed survey results make an important contribution to these strategies by providing descriptive information about the current collections and services provided in the major American research universities. This information is presented as a series of profiles that characterize the funding, the scope and depth of the materials held, the range of services provided, and the historical evolution of these collections. This information defines more sharply the diversity of resources available to support Japanese studies.

This descriptive information is essential for changing and improving these collections. On a broad interinstitutional scale the case can be made for selective strengthening of individual libraries to serve as centers for development and cooperative access. Concurrently, the information can be applied to internal problem-solving and improvement. The notion, for example, of focusing smaller collections on support of instructional programs and relying on larger collections for research backup can be advanced with these profiles. The individual library is also able to compare and relate its resources to collegial institutions in a consistent and uniform fashion.

Curators of Japanese collections also can take their own profiles and initiate more extensive internal studies. The strategy of tying future development of the collections to instructional needs of the university can be implemented by demonstrating the relationship among the content of the collection and the content of instructional offerings of the institutions. This relationship can be further analyzed by studying use patterns and user success in securing needed materials. Techniques for relating collections to programs, studying user patterns, determining level of user satisfaction and locating causes of user failure are presently available for academic libraries. The use of such techniques is predicated on sound descriptive information such as that provided here.

The future development of Japanese collections requires concerted efforts at both the local and national levels, with curators of these collections having a pivotal role. A philosophy of collaboration with colleagues and support of a strategic approach to these common dilemmas faced by Japanese collections is essential. This report provides better information to advance this collaborative strategy.

December 1980   Duane E. Webster

Introduction

The primary aim of this survey has been to research the present status of Japanese collections in the United States and to suggest directions for their future growth. The Japanese collections treated here exist as special collections within East Asia or Asia libraries at American universities, and these in turn usually include Chinese, Japanese, Korean and other minor language materials. These collections were established for the most part in support of Japanese Studies Programs and, with the exceptions of the Library of Congress, and the Harvard, Yale, Columbia and Northwestern University libraries, all of them were founded after World War II.

During the 1960's, when general interst in Asian Studies was high and the American economy strong, the Japanese collections grew rapidly both in size and number. By the late 1970's the international economic situation had changed the value of the dollar relative to the inflated yen, so that by 1980, the purchasing power of the American dollar in Japan had decreased by at least 25%. In practical terms this means that a book budget of $10,000 in 1970 would be worth only $6,000 in 1980, not considering overseas mailing costs which have trebled during the same period.

In spite of these financial strains the Japanese collections enjoyed continued growth through the end of the 70's, due to increased funding from a number of sources—their host university libraries, American and Japanese foundations and individual donors, and the Japan-U.S. Friendship Commission. The total amount of money spent by the twenty-seven university libraries for the purchase of Japanese monographs in 1979-80 was about $1,080,522. Funds for serials are generally paid by the Serial Departments and the exact amount devoted to Japanese materials is not available, but probably 1/4 should be added to the amount spent on monographs. The minimum total may then be estimated at around $1,084,844. Expressed in terms of books, the increase in the number of volumes in the same twenty-seven libraries over the past five years, 1975-1980, was 262,447 volumes, an average of 1944 volumes per year per library.

This rapid growth was necessary to meet the needs of expanded programs of Japanese Studies, whose increase continued through the past decade. The dispersion of specialists on Japan to new colleges and universities; expansion of already existing programs into professional schools such as business, law and journalism; outreach programs in elementary and high schools; undergraduate core courses; upper-level interdisciplinary courses; new graduate degrees and integration of graduate and professional degree programs: all these mark the trend for the 1980's.* Japanese Studies, while remaining part of the standard academic education in the humanities and social sciences, have come to be a part of increasingly diverse segments of American education, and thus of American culture. This is a great achievement and a source of justifiable pride for the professionals whose library collections have supported this growth of influence.

Thus, libraries in the 1980's may expect to face increasing demands to build their collections to accomodate the new disciplines of professional schools and outreach programs. However, it is impossible for libraries to provide coverage of new fields and subjects without extra funding for the purpose, because, large and small, they are trying to make ends meet while adding as many new publications as possible to maintain the usefulness of their existing collections. Knowing that money is scarce, and feeling the pressures created by the needs of their users, their administrators are obliged to do their best under often difficult circumstances.

Though this survey is not exhaustive in its scope or detail, its project coordinator feels it was made at a particularly significant time. The beginning of the 1980's is clearly a period in which we should review our individual situations as the keepers of the Japanese collections and consolidate our plans for the future, the better to share what we already have and to acquire what we still lack, so that Japanese collections, not individually, but as a whole, can progress and meet the expanding needs of their users. With this goal in mind, the survey report was compiled in the following order:

1) A profile of each collection, including its background, current organization, and special strengths.
2) Observations and issues affecting the various collections.

Acknowledgements

This survey project of Japanese collections in the United States was made possible by a grant from the Japan-U.S. Friendship Commission. Its executive director, Mr. Francis B. Tenny, and the project consultants, Dr. Warren Tsuneishi of the Library of Congress, Mr. Hisao Matsumoto, Japanese Section, Library of Congress, Mr. Hideo Kaneko of Yale university, and Mr. Weiying Wan of the University of Michigan, each gave me encouragement and thoughtful advice. All the librarians of East Asia libraries, especially those in

---

* <u>Culcon Report on Japanese Studies at Colleges and Universities in the United States in the Mid-70's.</u> By Elizabeth T. Massey and Joseph A. Massey. 1977. 141p.

charge of Japanese collections, supported the survey willingly and supplied the information I needed. Without their generous attention and cooperation this survey could not have been made, and I hope this report will benefit these same librarians in strengthening their collections.

A special acknowledgement goes to Mr. Duane Webster, Director of the Office of Management Studies of the Association of Research Libraries for his analysis of the survey, valuable comments and advice and who kindly wrote a foreword for this survey. Mr. Webster directed the first workshop for Japanese librarians in 1978.

Finally, the Center for Japanese Studies at the University of Michigan, its office staff, and especially Mrs. Elsie L. Orb, administrative assistant, Mr. Paul Grams and Ms. Tramell Ridgell who produced the copy for printing, Mr. Allan Doyle for editorial assistance and Reiko Bradley and Sharalyn Orbaugh for secretarial help; to all these I would like to acknowledge with grateful thanks.

August 1980   Naomi Fukuda

Explanatory Notes

1. Statistics

The project coordinator visited 30 university libraries, four law libraries, and the Library of Congress over a period of one and a half years, from January 1979 to July 1980. This report covers 28 of those libraries; those excluded from the report had holdings of only several hundred books purchased for Japanese language professors, and a few of the collections are dormant at present.

The figures in the report have been compiled as accurately as possible. Each library supplied the number of holdings and uncataloged items, budget, acquisitions and cataloging information, etc., while the coordinator counted titles by inspecting the shelf lists. In the process of checking through the shelf list, when analytical entries followed the series entry card, each entry was counted, as this gives easier access to the collection. Also, some special topics were chosen as the basis with which to compare coverage and probable strength within those topics between libraries. Some of these topics are Buddhism, local history, individual works (such as the Manyoshu and the Genji Monogatari), and bibliographical and critical works of some modern authors published in monographic works (see Appendix 6).

The time lag in the actual survey of the 28 libraries creates as much as one and a half year difference in the statistical bases used for comparison.

The Texas collection report, for instance, was based on a January, 1979 visit, while Pennsylvania was surveyed in January, 1980, and Minnesota in July, 1980. The figures given for each library are correct for the time of the visit, but the early data have not been updated for most of the libraries. Therefore, I decided to use the data as they stood to find the probable total figures. Discrepancies in these totals can theoretically be corrected by adding the annual or semi-annual increase in books, but the use of these supposed figures may lead to greater inaccuracies than simply using the available data. Therefore, having the year of the survey indicated when necessary, the original figures were taken as an indicator of the present state of affairs.

2. Statistical Tables
    1) Resources - alphabetical
    2) Annual growth - alphabetical
    3) Funding - alphabetical
    4) Geograhical distribution
    5) General status - by size
    6) Select topics by holding libraries

3. Classification Systems

    There are three main classification systems currently in use in the United States—the Harvard-Yenching, Nippon Decimal, and the Library of Congress. Except for the Harvard-Yenching Library, which originated its own system and is still using it, all other libraries use, or are converting to, the Library of Congress classification. These different systems have been expanded from time to time by their own compilers, but often libraries continued to use the system in its original form, making their own modifications. Quite often one book will be cataloged within different classes in different libraries. Here, for convenience of comparison, the systems were all adapted to the Library of Congress classifications, and the numbers of titles were transferred to L.C. subject divisions. In the strictest statistical sense, the figures herein may be questionable for some divisions, but the adaptation of classes was planned to be as consistent as possible, so the figures may be taken reliably to show an accurate distribution of books by subject.

4. Circulation

    Most of the larger libraries, especially those housed in a separate building from the main university library, are responsible for administering the circulation of their books, while for others the main library handles circulation. It follows that a number of university libraries have no circulation record for Japanese books. In any case it is difficult to compare circulation figures, since 1) some libraries are open 40 hours per week while others keep the hours of their main libraries—usually 90 hours per week, and 2) some librarians ask users to check out books whenever they take them from the stacks, while others keep records only for the use of books outside the library.

5. Date of Establishment

Since Japanese collections are usually included in larger East Asian libraries, the dates given here for their establishment may indicate either the year when Japanese books were acquired for the first time, or more often, when the first collections of Chinese books marked the beginning of an East Asian library.

6. Number of faculty members and enrollment figures

A special report by Massey (re: Culcon Report on Japanese Studies... referred in the introduction) describes the situation clearly. Mobility of professors vs. permanent number of professors is confusing when they are listed in university circulars for certain years, one in their permanent universities and the other as a visiting professor. Therefore, the number of professors in this survey means the number for the year the library was surveyed.

There were no current enrollment figures for East Asia or Japanese studies for several of the universities. When the figures were available they have been included in the "background information" with explanatory notes as needed. When enrollment figures were not available from the university, no attempt was made to estimate them.

7. "Uncataloged" items

"Uncataloged" or "pre-cats" mean items which are not fully cataloged. In most libraries these are listed briefly so that they are made available for users when necessary.

8. Abbreviations

AAS	Association for Asian Studies
ARL	Association of Research Libraries
DC	Dewey Decimal Classification
EA	East Asia
est.	estimate
grads	graduate students
H-Y	Harvard Yenching
JPTC	Japan Publications Trading Company
L.C.	Library of Congress
mos	months
NDC	Nippon Decimal Classification
NDL	National Diet Library (of Japan)
NUC	National Union Catalog
OCLC	Ohio College Library Center
precats	uncataloged books
UCB	University of California at Berkeley
UCLA	University of California at Los Angeles
UCSB	University of California at Santa Barbara

UNIVERSITY OF ARIZONA
at Tucson

Oriental Studies Collection

University of Arizona at Tucson, Oriental Studies Collection
Established in 1964
Tucson, Arizona 85721

I. Background
    Faculty: 6
    Graduate students: 10 Japanese studies majors
    Undergraduates: 23 Japanese studies majors

II. Organization
1. Location: Fifth floor of University's Science Library
2. Holdings:
    a) <u>Monographs</u>: 23,125 volumes, including 2,000 uncatalogued volumes, or 7,675 titles in 21,125 volumes.
    Major subject distribution in percentages:
    Hist. = 24%   Lang. & Lit.= 27%   Soc. Sci. = 19%

80% L.C. Classification, 20% H-Y	Titles
General works, Bibliography	211
Philosophy, Religion	634
History	1,815
Japanese History, 1,026	
Social Science, Economics	965
Political Science	274
Law	89
Education	112
Music	
Fine Arts	339
Language & Literature	2,035
Japanese Language, 371	
Japanese Literature, 1329	
Science & Technology	295
Military Science	23
Total	6,792
plus titles acquired in 1980	883
Grand Total	7,675

    b) <u>Microfilms</u>: 16 titles on 137 reels
    c) <u>Serials</u>: Periodical subscriptions, 150 titles; newspaper subscriptions, 6
    d) <u>Slides</u>: 4 titles on 500 slides
3. Staff: 1.5 professionals, 1 paraprofessional, student help. Staff reports to the Oriental Collection Head, who reports to the Director of the University Libraries.

III. Collection Management
1. Classification system: 80% Library of Congress, 20% Harvard-Yenching. In the process of reclassifying H-Y to L.C.
2. Shelving of books: separated by language
3. Public catalog: separated by language
4. Book selection: recommendations by professors and Japanese staff

5. Acquisitions: information not available
6. Cataloging: 1978-79, 682 titles in 1,311 volumes (includes recataloged items); 1979-80, 883 titles in 1,400 volumes.
7. Circulation: Automated system for the entire library (GEAC). Open hours, reference staff and services: M - F, 8 am - 5 pm. Sample circulation figures not available.
8. Financing:

a) <u>Book budget</u>:

University funds (includes serials)		$26,200
Outside funds		5,000
Total		$31,200
(100 gift books received in 1979/80)		

b) <u>Staff salaries</u>: 2.75 staff $38,002

University of Arizona at Tucson   January 1979, revised July 1980

The Oriental Collection is located on the 5th floor of the University's Science Library. The collection houses the Chinese, Japanese, Arabic, Persian, Hindi, Urdu, Turkish and other Oriental language books, periodicals and newspapers, while Western language materials are located in the University Library's main collection. Microforms are housed with those of the Science Library for the convenience of users.

Due to its geographical location, the University is a member of the AAS Southwest Rocky Mountain Regional Conference. As the oldest of the three state universities, it maintains a close relationship with Arizona State University at Tempe, which has 3 faculty members in Japanese language and literature and others in various departments such as art history, history, political science, religion, etc. The library has a shuttle bus service to Tempe twice a week.

The Oriental Collection functions as a reference and acquisition section, while cataloging is done by Technical Services. The Collection is administered by a Middle East and South Asia specialist as its head, along with a Chinese professional and a Japanese professional. Cataloging is done by a Chinese professional in Technical Services. His duties include not only the cataloging of new books, but also the reclassifying of volumes from the Harvard-Yenching to the Library of Congress classification whenever time permits. About 80 percent of the Japanese collection has been reclassified to the Library of Congress system.

Each language section keeps an author-title-subject catalog. For the convenience of the staff, the Japanese section maintains a shelf list and statistical tables to record each acquisition by subject.

UNIVERSITY OF CALIFORNIA
at Berkeley

East Asiatic Library

University of California at Berkeley, East Asiatic Library
Established in 1896
Berkeley, California 94720

I. **Background**
    Faculty members: 20, plus 8 visiting scholars, and 5 research staff.
    Enrollment for East Asian studies: 2,759 undergraduates; 265 graduates
    Enrollment for Japanese studies: less than 55% of above figures

II. **Organization**
1. Location: Main holdings and library offices in Durant Hall, Berkeley campus; other subjects in Life Sciences Building; less-used subjects stored in Richmond, California.

2. Holdings:
    a) <u>Monographs</u>: 189,575 volumes, including 2,728 uncataloged but already accessioned volumes and 39,974 (estimated) unaccessioned and uncataloged volumes. 54,570 titles in 146,873 volumes.
    <u>Major subject distribution in percentages:</u>
    Hist. = 22%   Lang. & Lit.= 23%   Soc. Sci. = 29%

<u>H-Y Classification adapted to L.C.</u>	<u>Titles.</u>
General works, Bibliography	3,395
Philosophy, Religion	4,733
Buddhism, 1,943	
History, Geography	12,178
Japanese History, 7,222	
Social Science, Economics, Sociology	11,428
Political Science	2,493
Law	780
Education	1,139
Music	175
Fine Arts	2,620
Language & Literature	12,693
Japanese Language, 1,881	
Japanese Literature, 9,161	
Science, Technology, & Military Science	2,936
Total	54,570

    b) <u>Microfilm</u>: 2,143 reels
    c) <u>Microfiche</u>: 2,226 sheets
    d) <u>Periodicals</u>: 1,733 titles by purchase, gifts, and exchange
    e) <u>Newspapers</u>: 17 titles, 1 by airmail

3. Staff: 2.5 professionals (one position vacant, 1979/80), 2.25 clericals, 5 others. Staff reports to Director of East Asiatic Library, who is directly under the University librarian.

III. **Collection Management**
1. Classification system: All new items since January 1980 by L.C. classification if an L.C. card is available; all others by H-Y system.
2. Shelving of books: Chinese, Japanese and Korean are intershelved.
3. Public catalog: Formerly, EA language entries were interfiled in a radical-stroke catalog. An alphabetical author-title catalog is currently replacing this system.
4. Book selection: Japanese bibliograher, recommendations of professors
5. Acquisitions: Monographs   1973-77   15,365 vols.
                                              1977-78   4,606 vols.
                                              1978-79   4,138 vols.
                Bound serials, 1978-79   1,204 vols.
                Serial subscriptions   titles added: 36
                                              titles cancelled: 24
6. Cataloging: 1977-78, 1,774 titles (L.C. cards = 778, original = 946); 1978-79, 1,806 titles (L.C. cards = 1,246, original = 560)
7. Circulation: Open hours: M - F, 8 am - 5 pm; Sat 9 am - 5 pm.
Sample circulation figures: 983 titles during 6 months, 367 by students, 547 by faculty/staff, 31 by visitors, and 29 interlibrary loans. Subject distribution:

	No. of Items
Humanities	
History	458
Lang. & Lit.	315
Art	110
Social Science and Others	100
Total	983

8. Financing:
   a) <u>Book budget</u>:

University Library book fund for Japan	$23,770
University Library subscription fund (est.)	34,576
Outside funds	36,756
Total	$95,102

(Average price of monographs, ¥4,546 or $19.43 for 1977-78)
   b) <u>Salaries</u>: Estimated Total for 4.75 staff $115,000
   c) <u>Other expenses</u>: Current acquisition list (bimonthly) paid by the University Library. Binding annual allocation, $3,500. Travel: approval for funding must first be granted by the University Library. Transportation costs are ususally paid in full. Perdiem is not always included.

University of California at Berkeley   June 1980

    The Japanese collection at Berkeley numbers some 200,000 volumes, about half the University's East Asiatic Library, and as such represents one of the largest Japanese collections in the United States. The library was founded in 1947 under the directorship of Dr. Elizabeth Huff, who co-ordinated extensive and important initial acquisitions in the early post-war years.

These include the Murakami Bunko—9,000 volumes of the Meiji period[1]; and the Mitsui Bunko—100,000 volumes, containing Edo and Meiji maps—2,000 items[2]; pre-1870 manuscripts, some 7,000 volumes[3]; and pre-1660 imprints—900 volumes.[4]

A survey of the collection shows comprehensive coverage in the humanities and social sciences, and, where economic and social conditions are concerned, in the applied sciences. Materials on local history are extensive and cover diverse subjects such as bibliographies, climate, political conditions, etc. Collections in the areas of literature, fine arts, and political science are especially distinguished.

The library is designated as the West Coast Depository Center for Japanese government publications and regularly receives a number of titles from the National Diet Library. (A complete set of Japanese government publications is deposited in the Library of Congress.) Also, many Japanese universities send their periodical publications to Berkeley in exchange for University of California publications, making the collection a periodical center for its area of the country.

Because of their size the collections of the East Asiatic Library are divided among three physical locations according to subject. The main holding, and the library offices, are housed in Durant Hall on the Berkeley campus; other subjects are kept in the Life Sciences Building and still others, less used, are kept in storage in Richmond, about one half hour's time from Berkeley by campus bus.

A short history of the library's organization helps to make clear certain changes now under way that affect the use of the collection. The first director emphasized a central unified organization, both for the East Asiatic collection itself, and among the library staff. Books in the several languages were interfiled in a radical stroke catalog and, instead of completely independent language sections, the functional model of organization provided that the various language specialists co-ordinated their efforts in at least some areas, through a chief of cataloging and a head for reference and acquisitions. This system remained essentially in force following Dr. Huff's retirement in 1968, until February, 1979 when Dr. Richard Cooper was appointed acting administrative director. Since then, both acquisitions and cataloging of Japanese materials have come under the jurisdiction of the Japanese division, one of five new sections in the East Asiatic Library, the others being Chinese, Korean, public service, and post-cataloging.

Corresponding changes had been made even earlier within cataloging systems. Since 1973, new acquisitions have been filed in an alphabetical author-title catalog, while the materials already in the radical-stroke catalog are being brought gradually into the newer one. Also, since January 1980, the Library of Congress classification has been followed for all new materials carrying L.C. cards, while all other materials will continue to be classified according to the Harvard-Yenching system.

In 1973 the library published a set of author-title catalogs of Japanese materials acquired up to that time. These were a counterpart to similar Chinese author-title catalogs arranged by radicals, and included a particularly useful checklist of periodical holdings. Later, a two-volume supplement to the author catalog was published arranged in alphabetical order, which has made the radical stroke catalog more accessible to users of the library. There is also a set of subject catalogs for Chinese, Japanese and Korean books. The changes currently being experienced at the Berkeley East Asiatic Library should not distract current and potential users of the Japanese collection from the fact of its basic excellence, both in number and quality of volumes. The auspicious period of its founding has been followed by years of successful acquisitions policy, ensuring its place among the foremost Japanese collections in the United States.

Bibliography

Regents of the University of California, Berkeley. nd. Elizabeth Huff: teacher and founding curator of the East Asiatic Library, with an introduction by John C. Jamieson.

Sherman, Roger. 1980. The acquisition of the Mitsui collection by the East Asiatic Library, University of California, Berkeley. Essay submitted in partial fulfillment of the requirements for the MLS degree, UCLA.

Yutani, Eiji. 1976. Japanese rare books and special collections in the East Asiatic Library, University of California, Berkeley: A preliminary survey. Mimeographed.

Publications

The East Asiatic Library:
    The Collections; Services. 1979. Mimeographed. 2p.
    The Catalogs. 1979. Mimeographed. 3p.

The East Asiatic Library. nd. Flyer.

Enrollments in East Asian Studies at UCB. 1979. Mimeographed. 1p.

Notes:

(Excerpted from <u>Japanese Rare Books and Special Collections in the East Asiatic Library</u>... by Eiji Yutani. p.3-8.)

1. The Murakami Library

The Murakami Library (or Murakami Bunko) contains writings of Japanese men of letters and ideas who made their reputations during the Meiji period (1868-1912). The Library consists of approximately 9000 volumes, and is noteworthy for the number of first editions it contains (although we do not have statistics available on the exact number). We believe that the collection has no rival outside Japan, and few, if any, there.

For example, noted works by Mori Ogai like <u>Minawashū</u> (1892), <u>Maihime</u> (1907), are first editions. So are Natsume Sōseki's <u>Kokoro</u> (1914) and <u>Meian</u> (1917). The collection is rich in works of poetry and essays as well as of fiction and drama. For instance, Shimazaki Tōson's <u>Wakanashū</u> (1897) and Nagai Kafū's <u>Amerika Monogatari</u> (1908), to name only a few.

I would like to emphasize that the collection contains not only works of belles lettres, but also writings on social and political problems of the time, including important translations of Western books. You will find in the collection Fukuzawa Yukichi's <u>Gakumon no susume</u> (1871), and Inoue Tetujirō's <u>Kyōiku to shūkyō no shōtotsu</u> (1893). As for translations, we have Nakamura's <u>Jiyū no ri</u>, a translation of John Stuart Mills' <u>On Liberty</u> (1871), and Nakae Chōmin's <u>Minyaku yakukai</u>, a translation of J.J. Rousseau's <u>Social Contract</u> (1882), and many more. Again, all of these are first edition publications. It is unfortunate that Mr. Murakami, the original collector, did not collect as many works by Higuchi Ichiyō as we might wish, but except for this woman novelist, it appears that the collection contains important works by all major writers of the Meiji period.*

We may measure the monetary value of these materials by examining current market prices listed in the latest old book catalogues. For instance, I have recently noticed the first edition of <u>Gakumon no susume</u>, previously mentioned, at a price of 100,000 Yen, a single early Meiji work for $300 U.S., as of December, 1975.

* Some years ago Professor Muramatsu of Sophia University, the foremost authority on the Meiji novelist Izumi Kyōka, examined some 50 volumes on Kyōka and showed his high praise for the quantity and quality of them. Professor Irokawa of Tokyo College of Economics, a leading historian on the Jiyū Minken movement did the same for the collection in his research field.

2. Edo and Meiji Maps

Our old map collection consists of some 2000 maps. They are maps chiefly of the 17th through 19th centuries, printed for the most part from wood-blocks (many in color), or engraved copper plates. We believe that in size and quality the collection is rivaled by only a few collections in Japan. It is my personal view that perhaps maps of Edo, numbering about 200, are the best and most valuable of all.

The collection is divided into eight geographical areas and two subjects. They are: (1) the world, (2) East Asia, (3) Japan proper, (4) Provinces and prefectures, (5) Edo and Tokyo, (6) Kyoto, (7) Osaka, (8) other cities, (9) Meisho zue (pictorial maps of noted places), and (10) Dōchū (travel maps). The number of maps for each category are as follows: the world, 68; East Asia, 67; Japan proper, 211; provinces and prefectures, 408; Edo and Tokyo, 421; Kyoto, 205; Osaka, 126; other cities, 369; Meisho zue, 42; and travel maps, 72.

We may also characterize the collection in terms of periods, namely, pre-1868 and post-1868. We have 267 maps which were printed before 1868, thus constituting about 16 percent of the total. The remaining 1,627 maps, or about 84 percent, belong to the post-1868 period. I would like to add, however, that about half of the Edo and Tokyo maps, one-third of Japan proper, Kyoto and Osaka, and one-fourth of the world maps are pre-1868 maps. The oldest of all maps seems to be the Osaka map of 1656. The oldest map in each area following that Osaka map may be enumerated in the following chronological order: 1666: Japan; 1676: Edo; 1670's: Kyoto; 1710: World; 1770: travel map; 1835: China; 1853: province (Hokkaido).

In terms of printing methods, my preliminary survey shows the following ratio: 33 percent for wood-block; 48 percent for copper-plated engraving; 10 percent for lithographs, and 9 percent with movable type text. In order to give some indication of the monetary value of the collection, I would like to mention the current market price for one single map offered by a London map dealer. In his recent catalog of foreign maps, an 1810 map of the world, Shintei Bankoku Zenzu, is listed at the price of 2,000 British pounds. Our collection does not happen to include this particular one.

3. Manuscripts

The manuscript collection consists of some 7,000 volumes, of which almost all are pre-20th century, and an as yet unknown number of holographs. Most of these materials are in cursive writing, and the subjects dealt within them are apparently quite wide and diverse, ranging from Renga through Shogunal ordinances. Therefore, they are still an untapped mine which only trained and experienced specialists can analyze and process.

I would like to give you a mere glimpse of what is available in this mine of valuable original sources. I have selected five manuscripts of Meiji and Taisho writers whose literary achievements are familiar to us. Among these five, two—namely Akutagawa Ryūnosuke's Haha (Mother), 1921, and Osanai Kaoru's Yoakemae (Before dawn)—are printed in journals or in their collected works. The other three are not found in any printed source and are therefore unpublished pieces of work and available only in our rare book collection. They are Kōda Rohan's essay on flower arrangement (n.d.), Tsubouchi Shōyō's treatises on Kabuki theatre (1924), and Musakoji Saneatsu's novel, Nara o tatsu mae (Before leaving the city of Nara; 1926).

A group of Japanese scholars from Nihon University visited our library last summer and examined some of these manuscripts for three days. After their survey Professor Tomotarō Suzuki, an authority on Heian literature, reported that at least part of the collection in court poetry and monogatari is excellent, although the group did not find many which may be regarded as important cultural properties, let alone "national treasures." But they selected 16 titles in 37 volumes as extremely valuable materials, all of which were copied in the early or middle Edo period.

4. Pre-1660 Japanese imprints

Japanese imprints housed in our "rare book room" consist of some 900 volumes. As I have mentioned before, our cut-off year for classifying printed materials as "rare" is 1660. We have some 15 titles in 735 volumes which were engraved before 1660. If we exclude the 8th century hyakumantō darani, the earliest Japanese xylograph, of which one copy is kept in the room, the oldest of these pre-1660 materials is the Mahaprajna-paramitasutra of 1384, consisting of 600 folding books. The subjects dealt within them are mainly Buddhism, Japanese and Chinese poetry and fiction. In addition, there are many post-1660 imprints, which we have put in the room because of their intrinsic value. Among them are 7 titles in 11 volumes which were printed between 1661 and 1669. They deal with waka, haiku, and biography. We have a one-volume literary work which came out in 1730.

The earlier 19th century "rare" imprints are more numerous, however. You will find in the room some 15 titles in 85 volumes, all printed between 1802 and 1865. The range of subjects in them is rather wide—Buddhism, history, Korea, language and literature, maps, tobacco and whaling. Moreover, we have some 25 woodcut pictures of Otsue and Shokunin zue, which were probably printed in the early 19th century. Although some 20th century rarities also occupy shelves in the room, I have omitted them in this discussion.

Joint Project of Univerity of California (Berkeley) and Hoover Institution
June 1979

In order to facilitate the use of resources in their libraries the two universities compiled and published the following three lists:

1) <u>A Checklist of Japanese Local Histories:</u> Study sponsored by Japan-United States Friendship Commission. East Asiatic Library, University of California at Berkeley and East Asian Collection, Hoover Institution (Stanford-Uniersity) 1978. 312p. (East Asia Library Series 1)
2) <u>A Checklist of Japanese Company Histories:</u> Study sponsored by Japan-United States Friendship Commission... 1978. 92p. (East Asia Library Series 2)
3) <u>A Checklist of Japanese Newspapers:</u> Study... 1978. 22p. (East Asia Library Series 3)

The above three publications are studies based on findings of the extent to which the two libraries duplicated their respective holdings.

The possibility has recently been discussed of the Hoover and Berkeley Asia libraries coordinating their acquisitions of new books. The advantage would be to lessen new book costs by reducing the number of duplicate titles in the two libraries, which serve essentially the same geographical area, and which are already mutually accessible through a special bus service between the two campuses. The plan offers the specific advantage of the Hoover Library of allowing it to concentrate its resources on maintaining and enlarging its highly specialized collection, while the weight of comprehensive coverage would remain with Berkeley, with its already broadly based collection.

UNIVERSITY OF CALIFORNIA
at Los Angeles

Oriental Library

University of California at Los Angeles, Oriental Library
Established in 1948
405 Hilgard Ave., Los Angeles CA 90024

I. Background
Faculty members: 13
Enrollment: no data available
II. Organization
1. Location: Second floor of Research Library
2. Holdings: 1978
    a) <u>Monographs:</u> 71,200 volumes, including 7,000 uncataloged volumes. 15,353 titles in 64,000 cataloged volumes. 71,200 represents an estimate, since books are stored in various places; the total number of books, by actual count, might be much lower.
    <u>Major subject distribution in percentages:</u>
    Hist. = 25%   Lang. & Lit.= 27%   Soc. Sci. = 21%

	L.C.	H-Y	Total
General works, Bibliography	226	620	846
Philosophy	110	183	293
Religion	140	105	245
Buddhism	403	921	1324
Other religions	43	114	157
Auxiliary Science of History	119	651	770
History—general, China	125	300	425
Japanese History	1122	1280	2402
Korea and others	242	33	275
Social Science, Economics	587	840	1427
Sociology	236	543	779
Politics and Law	211	494	705
Education	142	116	258
Language and Literature, China	13	99	112
Language, Japan	157	425	582
Literature, Japan	1278	1968	3246
Drama, criticism	117	28	145
Music	12	45	57
Fine Arts	410	783	1193
Science, Technology, Mil. Sci.	112		112
Total titles	5805	9548	15,353

   b) <u>Microfilm:</u> 8 titles on 190 reels
   c) <u>Periodical subscriptions:</u> 146 titles
   d) <u>Newspaper subscriptions:</u> 4 titles
   e) <u>Pamphlet files:</u> 120 titles
3. Staff: 1 professional, .5 paraprofessional, .3 student. Staff handles its own circulation, acquisition, and cataloging. Budget, personnel and collection development are handled by other University Library offices.

III. Collection Management

1. Classification system: 38% L.C., 62% H-Y
2. Shelving of books: Shelf lists divided into L.C. and H-Y; within this division, Asian language books are intershelved.
3. Public catalog: cards filed separately by language
4. Book selection: recommendations by professors and Japanese librarian
5. Acquisitions:

	Monographs	1973-77	7,129 vols.
		1977-78	2,062 vols.
		7/78-12/78	315 vols.
	Serials	1973-77	142 titles
	(24 added, 16 cancelled)		
		1977-78	138 titles
	(8 added)		

6. Cataloging: 1977-78, 995 titles in 2295 volumes (by L.C. cards, 553; originals, 371; recataloging, 93)
7. Circulation: Open hours: M - F, 8 am - 5 pm

Sample circulation figures (Sept. - Dec., 1977)

By UCLA students	1,167 vols.
By UCLA faculty/staff	659 vols.
By visitors	278 vols.
Interlibrary loans	30 vols.
Total	2,136 vols.

Subject distribution

	Titles	Volumes
Humanities		
History	140	250
Lang. & Lit.	273	400
Art	75	130
Religion	350	575
Other	110	230
Social Sciences		
Economics	42	103
Politics	60	145
Sociology	51	123
Other	58	180

8. Financing: 1977-78

a) Book budget:

University Library, Japanese book fund	$14,289
University Library subscriptions serials, continuations	5,500
Outside funds (government)	7,500
Other gifts (money or books)	700
Total	$27,989
Average price of serial subscription per title	$30.00
Average price of continuation per volume	$11.00
Average price of monograph per volume	$11.00

b) Salaries: 1.8 Staff $23,689

University of California at Los Angeles   March 1979

The University of California at Los Angeles Oriental Library is located on the second floor of the Research Library. It serves the Chinese and Japanese Studies, and the Korean Studies offered at the University of Southern California, as UCLA has about 6,000 volumes on Korea. As a section of the Humanities Group of the Research Library, the Oriental Library is partitioned off from the general library area, and has its own service hours, from 8 a.m. to 5 p.m., Mondays through Fridays. It handles its own circulation, acquisition, cataloging, etc. For matters concerning budget, personnel, or collection development, it must deal with the offices in charge.

The stacks are open, rather full, and uncataloged books are stored in other places, though they are available for users upon request. The collection, 40 percent Japanese and 60 percent Chinese, was classified according to the Harvard-Yenching system until 1973, at which time the transition was begun to the Library of Congress classification. At present, 38 percent is by L.C and 62 percent by Harvard-Yenching, and the shelf lists are divided into two corresponding parts within which Chinese, Japanese and Korean books are interfiled. Books are also intershelved, though they are separated by language in the public catalog.

This library serves as the Center for Southern California East Asian Librarians Group, which includes University of California at Santa Barbara, Universty of Southern California, San Diego State University (which has a small Japanese collection), and Claremont College. Their librarians meet once a year to discuss the cooperative programs which includes: 1) exchange of original catalog cards; 2) exchange of duplicates; 3) exchange of serial lists. UCLA and UCSB are linked by bus service which runs once a day, 6 days a week, between the two.

It is interesting to note that the libraries in this area have more books on religion than is usually the case. The UCLA collection was started by Professor Ashikaga, now emeritus, who is an ordained priest, and it was also supported by a large Buddhist community in Los Angeles. UCSB emphasizes the study of religion, in accordance with the California universities' master plan. The Claremont College Library also has books on religion which are gifts from the neighboring Blaisdell Institute for the Study of World Religions and Cultures. The percentages of the collections on religion in each of the three libraries are as follows:

UCLA Religion	1,726 titles; 11% of total
(books on Buddhism	1,324 titles; 77% of above holdings)
UCSB Religion	329 titles; 7% of total
(books on Buddhism	142 titles; 43% of above holdings)
Claremont Religion	198 titles; 10% of total
(books on Buddhism	7 titles)

It is premature to assess the quality of these collections on religion, but certainly a union list of their collections by areas, especially a list on Buddhism for UCLA and UCSB, would bring about closer cooperation and could be used as a tool for future quality control. UCLA has 342 titles in 968 volumes and two scrolls of manuscripts of Mandara, used by Professor Shoun Toganoo (1881-1953), an internationally known scholar of Esoteric Buddhism.

Bibliography

Kim, Id-Sam. 1978. The oriental library. UCLA Librarian 31:29-31.

UNIVERSITY OF CALIFORNIA
at Santa Barbara

Oriental Collection

University of California at Santa Barbara, Oriental Collection
Established in 1967
Santa Barbara, California 93106

I. Background
Faculty: 13 in East Asian Studies, including 5 in Japanese studies.
Enrollment: no data available

II. Organization
1. Location: Fifth floor of the Research Library
2. Holdings:
    a) Monographs: 22,115 volumes, including about 604 uncataloged volumes; 6,494 titles in 21,511 cataloged volumes.

    Major subject distribution in percentages:
    Hist. = 28%   Lang. & Lit.= 29%   Soc. Sci. = 24%

L.C. Classification	Titles
General	583
Philosophy, Religion	585
History	1,818
Japanese History, 982	
Social Sciences	1,558
Language & Literature	1,883
Others	67
Total	6,494

    b) Microfilm: 1 title, 23 reels
    c) Microfiche: 1 title, 1,202 sheets (periodical back issue)
    d) Periodicals: about 5,000 bound volumes
    e) Serials: about 300 out of 342 are standing orders
3. Staff: 2 professionals, 1 paraprofessional, .6 student help (Oriental collection).

III. Collection Management
1. Classification system: L.C.
2. Shelving of books: languages are intershelved
3. Public catalog: cards are interfiled
4. Book selection: requests from professors and supplemental selections by Oriental Collection staff
5. Acquisitions: (estimates for Oriental Library)
    monographs (1975-80)   8,496 volumes, or 1,699 vols./yr.
    serial subscriptions (1979-80)   342 titles
6. Cataloging: (Japanese books only) 1977-78, 900 titles in 1,140 volumes (by L.C. and other library cards, 640; original, 260; recataloging, 15). 800 current titles uncataloged in 1977-78; 604 current titles uncataloged in 1978-79.
7. Circulation: Open hours: M - Th, 7:30 am - 11 pm; F, 7:30 am - 10 pm; Sa, 9 am - 10 pm; Su, 10 am - 11 pm.

8. Financing: (Oriental collection)
    a) Book budget:
        University Library, incl. serials $39,500
        (40/60 ratio of Japanese/Chinese)
    b) Salaries: 3.6 staff $62,800

University of California at Santa Barbara   March 1979; revised, June 1980

    The office of the Oriental Collection is located on the 5th floor of the Research Library, and has its stacks across the hall on the same floor. Begun only twelve years ago, it has already grown to be a sizable collection of 53,000 volumes, of which 40 percent are Japanese and 60 percent Chinese. At the time of this report it had one professional and one library assistant on its staff, with a few able clerical assistants, and one position open for a cataloger. The stacks are open during the same hours as those of the Research Library, and the circulation is handled by the general circulation desk. Japanese books are acquired upon requests from professors, with supplemental selections being made by the Oriental Collection staff.

    In addition to doing original cataloging, and adopting a certain percentage of catalog cards issued by the East Asiatic Library of UC Berkeley, the library bases its cataloging on the microfiche of the L.C. catalog cards, which are cumulated biweekly, annually, and so forth. To locate a volume, one first consults the indexes for author, title or card numbers to find the location of the desired entry on the main microfiche. The next step is to make an enlarged photocopy of the entry for reproducing it in card form. This system eliminates filing and waiting time for L.C. printed cards, and it serves this operation rather well.

    This library is a member of the Center for Research Libraries, and the Oriental Collection is a member of CEAL, the Association for Asian Studies, and the Southern California East Asian Librarians Group.

UNIVERSITY OF CHICAGO

Far Eastern Library

University of Chicago, Far Eastern Library
Established in 1936
Joseph Regenstein Library, 1100 E. 57th Street
Chicago, Illinois 60637

I. Background
Faculty: 13 Japan specialists, 6 East Asia specialists, 9 resident associates in the Chicago area.
Graduate students: Far East Area, 263 (49 Ph.D. candidates)
Undergraduates: Far East Area, 493

II. Organization
1. Location: Fifth floor of the Joseph Regenstein Library
2. Holdings:
    a) <u>Monographs</u>: 89,485 volumes, including 1,337 uncataloged volumes; 42,455 titles.
    <u>Major subject distribution in percentages:</u>
    Hist. = 25%   Lang. & Lit. = 28%   Soc. Sci. = 24%

H-Y Classification Adapted to L.C	.Titles)
General works, Bibliography	2,722
Philosophy	1,399
Religion	2,922
History	9,264
Japanese history, 4,680	
Japanese local history, 1,125	
Geography	1,442
Social Science, Economics	4,173
Sociology	2,360
Political Science	1,790
Law	775
Education	890
Music	125
Fine Arts	1,758
Language & Literature	11,725
Japanese Language, 1,500	
Japanese Literature, 2,699	
Science & Technology	905
Military Science	205
Total	42,455

    b) <u>Microfilms</u>: 50 titles in 630 reels
    c) <u>Periodicals</u>: 627 titles (20 titles are gifts)
    d) <u>Newspapers</u>: 10 titles
    e) <u>Pamphlets</u>: about 5,000 items
3. Staff: 3 professionals, 2.75 clericals, .4 student help. Head of Japanese section reports to head of Far Eastern Library, who is under the Associate Director of Reader Service.

III. Collection Management
1. Classification system: Harvard-Yenching
2. Shelving of books: separately by language
3. Public catalog: cards filed separately by language
4. Book selection: by Japanese bibliographer and Head of Japanese section, and by recommendations of professors. In 1977, formed a consortium with the University of Michigan Asia Library to coordinate book purchase of expensive items.
5. Acquisitions:

Total	1973-77	24,587 vols. (6,147/yr.)
	1977-78	4,476 vols.
	1978-79	3,584 vols.
Serials	1977-78	586 titles
	1978-79	627 titles

6. Cataloging: 1978-79, 3,104 titles in 3,502 volumes; added volumes 1,645. By L.C. cards, 1,459 titles; original cataloging, 557 titles in 1,120 volumes. Uncataloged monographs, 1,030 titles in 1,337 volumes; uncataloged serials, 186 titles in 1,325 issues.
7. Circulation: Open hours: M - Th, 9 am - 10 pm; F & Sa, 9 am - 5 pm. Sample circulation figures (Fall 1979, entire Far Eastern Library)

	Charges
Students and visitors	2,893
Faculty and staff	819
Interlibrary loan & photoduplication	83
Total	3,795
Estimated 40% Japanese	

8. Financing: 1978-79
   a) Book budget:

University Library allocation	$5,189.53
Endowment	2,742.52
Serials	11,332.50
Government funding	
HEW	7,027.33
Title IIC	10,275.33
Japan-U.S. Friends. Com.	14,163.21
Foundations	7,394.25
Total, 1978-79	$58,124.67
1977-78	57,519.60

Average price of monographs per volume = $20.71

   b) Salaries: 5.79 staff $77,527.19
   c) Other expenses: Monthly acquisitions list paid by general library and Center for Far Eastern Studies; binding paid by central budget; travel (airfare only) by central budget.

University of Chicago   July 1980

The Far Eastern Library at the Universty of Chicago was begun as a collection of Chinese books in 1936; Japanese materials were added beginning in 1958, and Korean and Western language books also later included. In 1978 Chinese materials comprised 66 percent and Japanese materials 26 percent of the total holdings.

The collections are housed on the 5th floor of the Joseph Regenstein Library; the facilities of the Far Eastern Library include a reading room with seating for 66, seminar rooms, typing and microfilm reading rooms, and a special stack area for rare books, with additionnal seating for 23 people.

Because of its location in the Chicago metropolitan area, the library enjoys the advantage of easy access to several nearby Japanese collections, many of them specialized. The Center for Research Libraries (CRL), of which the University of Chicago is a member, is located within walking distance.
The CRL is a cooperative library organized and supported by member libraries, and houses important but infrequently used materials, including Japanese statistical sources and archival materials, mostly on microfilm. Northwestern University houses the Oyama collection of over 13,000 volumes, which specializes in pre-war Japanese law and politics, and which is available for limited use upon request. The Ryerson Library of the Art Institute of Chicago is well known for its collection of Japanese prints. All these collections, while not technically part of the Far Eastern Library at the University of Chicago, still tend to enrich its holdings by their very proximity.

In 1977, the University's Far Eastern Library and the University of Michigan Asia Library formed a Midwest consortium to coordinate the selection and acquisition of Japanese books. The purpose of this consortium is to cooperate in the purchase of expensive items and to extend its services to other libraries in the region.

Bibliography

Tsien, T. H. 1956. Far Eastern Library of the University of Chicago, 1936-1956. Far Eastern Quarterly   656-58.

Publications

A brief guide to the Far Eastern Library. University of Chicago Library Reader Information Bulletin, no.7, revised 1978. 6p.

Author-title catalog of the Japanese collection. Boston: G. K. Hall, 1973. 4v.

Classified catalog and subject index of the Chinese and Japanese collections. Boston: G. K. Hall, 1973. 6v. (The supplement volumes will be published at the end of 1980.)

Daisaku Ikeda Collection of Japanese religion and culture, reference list 3. Far Eastern Library, 1977.

Far East: An exhibit of resources in the University of Chicago Library. 1973.

Far Eastern Library Annual Report.

Far Eastern Library circulation regulations. 1979. 4p.

Far Eastern Serials, reference list 2. Far Eastern Library, 1977.

Library handbook. University of Chicago Library, 1979.

Manual of technical processing and services. University of Chicago Library. Revised edition, 1978.

Occasional Report, no. 1-3. Far Eastern Library, 1977-1978 Newsletter.

Selective list of monthly acquisitions, no. 1. Far Eastern Library, 1978.

Selective list of recent Japanese acquisitions, no. 1-10. Far Eastern Library, 1961-1976.

Using the University of Chicago Library—Rules and metarules. University of Chicago Library, 1978. 8p.

COLUMBIA UNIVERSITY

East Asian Library

Columbia University, East Asian Library
Established in 1931
New York, New York 10027

I. Background
Faculty: 25
Graduate students: 106
Undergraduates: 204

II. Organization
1. Location: Kent Hall
2. Holdings:
   a) Monographs:

Cataloged	90,431 vols.
Partially cataloged	4,145 vols.
Title entry slips	5,473 vols.
Textbook, Emakimono, Go collections	3,329 vols.
Uncataloged and others	14,524 vols.
Total	117,902 vols.

(64,975 cataloged titles)

Major subject distribution in percentages:
Hist. = 29%   Lang. & Lit.= 21%   Soc. Sci. = 25%

NDC classification adapted to L.C.	Titles
General works, Bibliography	4,757
Philosophy	1,650
Religion	3,892
Buddhism, 2,598	
History	14,177
Japanese History, 5,259	
Geography	4,556
Social Science, Economics, Sociology	11,153
Political Science	1,924
Law	2,168
Education	1,315
Music	120
Fine Arts	2,817
Language & Literature	13,693
Japanese Language, 1,428	
Japanese Literature, 10,233	
Science & Technology	2,253
Military Science	490
Total	64,975

b) Microfilms: 1,729 reels
c) Serials: 800 current subscriptions; 32,294 bound volumes of periodicals; 6,497 government publications and bound volumes of newspapers.

d) Newspapers: 53 titles
e) Pamphlets: 1 cabinet (4 drawers) containing business reports of banks and companies.
f) Special collection of mathematics and geography: 755 volumes. Kept in Rare Book Room of the University Library, while its temporary catalog cards by title entry are in the East Asian Library.

Note: Columbia University Library counts bound periodicals separately from monographs. Therefore, its comparable total holdings, in volumes, is **156,693**.

3. Staff: 3 professionals, 2 paraprofessionals. Head of the Japanese section reports to head of the East Asian Library, who reports to the Vice President and University librarian.

III. Collection Management
1. Classification system: (L.C) NDC
2. Shelving of books: separately by language
3. Public catalog: cards interfiled
4. Book selection: by Head of East Asia Library, Japanese staff, and recommendations of professors
5. Acquisitions: Monographs   1974-77   13,002 vols.
                                     1977-78   3,407 vols.
                                     1978-79   3,693 vols.
6. Cataloging: 1978-79, 1,783 titles in 2,935 volumes (L.C. cards 100%).
7. Circulation: Open hours: M - Th, 9 am - 9 pm; F, 9 am - 5 pm; Sa, Noon - 5 pm.
Sample circulation figures (titles charged current July 8, 1980; shows about 1/3 of the average circulation data).

	Charges	Volumes
By students	398	499
By faculty/staff	291	356
By visitors	—	
Interlibrary loans	79	
Photoduplication	35	
Total	803	855

Subject distribution:

	Titles	Volumes
Humanities		
General	42	42
History	130	155
Language	33	38
Literature	127	93
Art	45	60
Religion/Thought	87	113
Others	123	123
Social Sciences		
Economics	41	50

Politics	28	28
Sociology	47	47
Law	20	20
Education	41	47
Commerce/Agric.	39	39
Totals	803	855

8. Financing: 1978-79
   a) <u>Book budget</u>:

University Library, Japanese books (including serials)	$59,915
Outside funds	21,598
Total	$81,513

   Gifts in books: 563 volumes

   b) <u>Salaries</u>: 5 staff $80,000
   1980-81: increase of one professional and one supporting staff member.

   c) <u>Other expenses</u>: Book binding, about $8,000 of East Asia Library's $12,000 binding budget is used for Japanese books. Travel funds are provided (often not in full) for 3 or 4 EAL staff members to annual AAS meeting. Other funds are available as occasion demands.

Columbia University   July, 1980

"Brief Background of the Formation of the Japanese Collection at Columbia"
Miwa Kai

Excerpts, May 8, 1980

The idea of creating a Japanese Cultural Center in New York having as its focal point a Japanese Library was formulated and implemented by Dr. Ryūsaku Tsunoda in 1927. With President Butler's support, a committee made up of professors from Columbia and Teacher's College was formed. Dr. Tsunoda then undertook to organize a comparable committee in Japan. With the support of these two committees, Dr. Tsunoda set forth on a campaign to solicit support in Japan.

Foremost among the early donors was Baron Iwasaki, Head of the Mitsubishi complex of companies, who donated funds to assemble a basic core collection as well as support to cover additional acquisitions and operational costs for a period of three years. Initial donors included the Imperial Household Library, central and local government offices, public and private libraries, universities, schools, and other educational institutions, leading business and banking concerns, newspaper and other media corporations, temples and shrines, national and private museums, and a host of private individuals.

Upon completion of the first three years, Columbia University offered to take over the responsibility of further development and maintenance...the Japanese collection joined the Chinese collection, established some two and a half decades earlier, to form the East Asiatic Collection, subsequently renamed the East Asian Library.

Thus, this Japanese collection owes its tradition of collection building as well as its founding to Dr. Ryūsaku Tsunoda (1877-1964). The East Asian Library was originally housed in Low Memorial Library, but was relocated in 1962 in the former Law School Library in Kent Hall. This present location features a large, high-ceiling reading room, distinctively decorated with antique oriental furniture and paintings; reference books are shelved on the surrounding mezzanine balcony. A staircase at the back of the circulation desk leads to four levels of stacks. At the time of this survey, the entire library was in the midst of renovation with plans for doubling the stack area.

The East Asian Library is designated as one of the Distinctive Collections of departmental libraries. Organized under four sections—Chinese, Japanese, Korean and Western Languages—it is headed by the East Asian Librarian, who reports directly to the University Librarian and Vice President. The responsibility of the Western Language section extends to appropriate materials on East Asian countries for all libraries on the campus, except for art, economics and business, and law. The section head is in charge of general readers' services, including circulation and bibliographical references.

The Japanese collection has a unique place in the University campus. Professor Tsunoda is remembered not only as the founder of the collection, but as a teacher and interpreter of Japanese culture to many students, and his rich legacy is apparent in the kinds of books he acquired for teaching and research while he was the curator of the Japanese Library. Visiting scholars and students from Japan also sought his guidance so that the University, through the medium of its Japanese Library, came to be something of an unofficial exchange center between the two countries.

This fact was recognized when the Japan Society of New York awarded the University a grant from the Rockefeller Foundation to establish a Committee of Intellectual Interchange between the United Stated and Japan soon after the Peace Treaty in 1952. Its purpose was to promote cultural exchange by inviting prominent scholars from Japan and the United States. A memorial book fund was established in Dr. Tsunoda's honor at the time of his death in 1964.

Miss Miwa Kai, who became Professor Tsunoda's assistant in 1945, is the present head of the Japanese collection under the East Asian Library. On the thirty-fifth anniversary of her service to the library, the Miwa Kai Anniversary Building Fund was established. Miss Kai's friendliness to visitors and devotion to the cause of better relations between the United States and Japan through library work could have no better place than at Columbia, situated at the crossroads of world culture. From the time of its founding the Japanese section has continued to receive many important materials as gifts from prominent Japanese alumni, making the collection notably favored in this respect.

CORNELL UNIVERSITY

Wason Collection

Cornell University, Wason Collection
Established in 1918
Ithaca, New York 14853

I. Background
Faculty: 7
Graduate students: 21 in East Asian studies
Undergraduates: 198 (EA)

II. Organization
1. Location: John M. Olin Library, first floor.
2. Holdings: 1979-80
    a) <u>Monographs</u>: 15,654 titles in 32,900 volumes. No uncataloged volumes. (Total includes 6,700 titles in 10,000 volumes of Japanese books on China, which are filed in alphabetical order, not by subject. In the following analysis, these books were omitted.)
    Major subject distribution in percentages:
    Hist. = 24%   Lang. & Lit.= 34%   Soc. Sci. = 17%

L.C. Classification	Titles
General works	435
Philosophy	150
Religion	350
History	1,906
Japanese History, 1,379	
Geography	250
Social Science, Economics, Sociology	1,061
Political Science	325
Law	50
Education	100
Music	50
Fine Arts	580
Language & Literature	3,070
Japanese Language, 425	
Japanese Literature, 2,343	
Science & Technology	185
Military Science	82
Bibliography	360
Total	8,954

   b) <u>Microfilm</u>: 4 titles on 1,360 reels
   c) <u>Serials</u>: 462 subscriptions, plus 956 retrospective titles
   d) <u>Newspapers</u>: 2 subscriptions (surface mail)
3. Staff: 1 professional, 1 paraprofessional, some student help. Staff reports to Assistant University Librarian for Collection Development.

III. Collection Management
1. Classification system: L.C.
2. Shelving of books: Chinese, Japanese intershelved
3. Public catalog: cards interfiled

4. Book selection: Head of the Wason Collection selects Western language books on East Asian countries. The East Asian Librarian selects books in the vernacular.
5. Acquisitions: Monographs: 1973-77, 7936 volumes; 1977-78, 1517 volumes; 1978-current, 848 volumes, 24 continuations, 215 serials-subscriptions.
6. Cataloging: 1977-78, 1,021 titles in 1,517 volumes (60% L.C. cards, 40% original cataloging)
7. Circulation: Open hours: 8 am - 10 pm daily.
   Sample circulation figures (February - May, 1979)

	No. of Charges	No. of Volumes
By students	326	364
By faculty/staff	138	170
By visitors	59	75
Interlibrary loan	7	8
Photoduplication	8	8
Total	538	625

Subject distribution:

	Titles	Volumes
Humanities		
History	75	94
Lang. & Lit.	271	303
Art	35	52
Religion	37	39
Other	6	6
Social Sciences		
Economics	52	63
Politics	16	18
Sociology	14	15
Other	32	35
Total	538	625

8. Financing: 1978-79
   a) Book budget:

University Library, Japanese book fund	$13,934
University Library, subscriptions/serials	8,464
Outside funds, foundations	7,000
Total	$29,398

   Remarks: Average price of serial subscriptions, $41 per title; average price of monographs, $20 per volume. Wason endowment is for material on China in Western languages; materials on Japan are added through University Library funds; in 1978-79 these amounted to $6,848.70.
   b) Salaries: 2 staff (FTE) and student help = $25,500 (est.)
      Remarks: The East Asia librarian is responsible for collection development and reference, while the East Asian cataloger is responsible for cataloging. Their combined work represents one full-time professional for the Japanese collection. The East Asian

assistant in the Serials Department, together with two part-time Japanese searchers, constitute one FTE also.

c) <u>Other expenses</u>: Weekly acquisition list in Chinese, Japanese, and Western languages for campus circulation is paid by Main Library. Travel expenses to annual professional meeting are usually shared by the China-Japan program and the University Library.

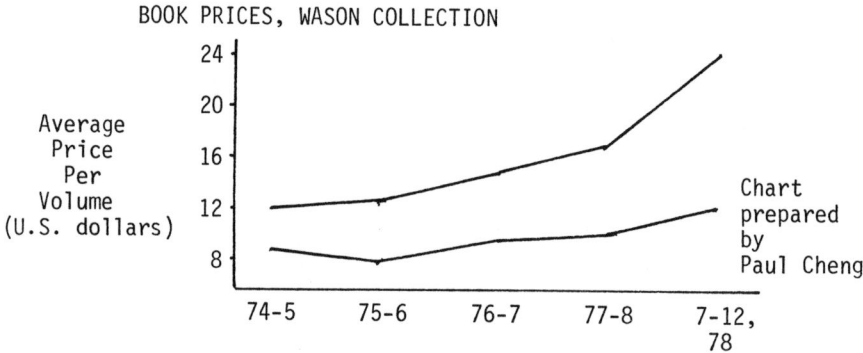

Cornell University, Wason Collection   May 1979; Rev. June 1980

  The Wason Collection serves the Asian Studies program at Cornell University and is divided into an East Asia collection and a Southeast Asia collection. The former houses books, periodicals, microfilms, etc., in vernacular Chinese, Japanese and Korean, as well as area studies of those countries in Western languages. The head of the Wason Collection reports to the University Librarian of the Cornell University Libraries, and is reponsible for selecting and buying Western language books on East Asian countries. The East Asian Librarian of the East and Southeast Asia collections both report to the Assistant University Librarian for Collection Development. They are responsible for acquiring vernacular language materials for their respective areas.

  Materials are processed by staff members of the catalog and serials sections of the general library; shelving of books is done by the stack service. Serials are checked, bound, and shelved by the sections responsible for each of these tasks, again within the general library. As a result, no separate record is kept of the number of bound volumes of current Japanese periodicals. Books displayed in the Wason Reading Room are processed by the Wason assistant. That there is no backlog of uncataloged books is testimony to the efficiency of the Library's cataloging section. The materials in the Wason Collection are included in the general library shelf lists, but the collection also keeps its own shelf lists divided by languages. Card for books on China in Japanese have been taken out temporarily for inclusion in the printed catalog of Chinese books, to be published by ARL's Center for Chinese Research Materials. These have not been counted by the surveyor, but are estimated to include about 6,700 titles in 10,000 volumes. A <u>locked place</u> in Wason stacks houses rare materials with post-1800 imprints. Pre-1800 imprints are kept in the Rare Book section of the Olin Library.

The Japanese Collection emphasizes works in the area of literature, reflecting the orientation of the teaching and research programs at the University. A program for religious studies, now in its second year, is being supported by the building of a basic collection of relevant materials, though at the time of this report there was neither a Japanese history specialist on the faculty, nor a Japanese bibliographer among the personnel of the Wason Collection.

The stacks are located within the caged area accessible through a check point in the Wason Reading Room. An open stacks system is followed, and the books are shelved according to the L.C. system. Within the general catalog, cards are filed by author, title, and subject, while the Wason collection maintains a catalog of main entry cards, interfiled word by word, of all languages.

Bibliography

Cheng, Paul P. W. 1974. Japanese Collection in Wason: A brief history and its current status. Mimeographed, supplements.

Cornell University Library. 1969. Special collection no.1: The Wason Collection. Ithaca, New York: Cornell University.

Ishikawa, Kazuo. 1978. The Rev. William Elliot Griffis Collection of old Japanese books at Cornell. Photocopied. Ithaca, New York: Center for International Studies, Cornell University. (535 items are listed with a short general introduction to the collection.)

Wolfe, Alan. 1980. The William Elliot Griffis Collection of old and rare Japanese books, Olin Library, Cornell University. <u>CEAL Bulletin</u> 63:40-47.

HARVARD UNIVERSITY

Harvard-Yenching Library

Harvard University, Harvard-Yenching Library
Established in 1879
2 Divinity Avenue, Cambridge, Massachusetts 02138

I. Background
Faculty: 27
Enrollment: figures not available

II. Organization
1. Location: Boylston Hall
2. Holdings:
    a) <u>Monographs</u>: 154,368 volumes (86,222 titles) in Harvard-Yenching Library, including about 1,000 uncataloged volumes; 13,000 volumes (7,482 titles) in Law School Library; 5,000 volumes (4,000 titles, est.) in Fogg Art Museum. Campus total: 173,183 volumes in 97,704 titles.

Major subject distribution in percentages:
Hist. = 23%   Lang. & Lit.= 24%   Soc. Sci. = 24%

Harvard-Yenching Library (H-Y Classification)	Titles
General works, Bibliography	5,318
Japanese works on China, 1,236	
Philosophy	3,455
Religion	8,728
Buddhism, 5,993	
History, Archaeology, Geography	19,610
Japanese Hist., etc., 9,672	
Social Science, general	581
Sociology and Social Conditions	4,801
Economics, Industry	5,886
Labor	934
Communications, Commerce	1,327
Finance	1,197
Political Science	2,862
Law	1,427
Education	1,677
Fine Arts, Music	4,066
Language & Literature	20,760
Japanese Language, 3,241	
Japanese Literature, 13,381	
Science & Technology	3,180
Military Science	413
TOTAL	86,222

    b) <u>Microfilm</u>: 1,587 reels
    c) <u>Periodicals</u>: 3,611 titles, including about 500 gift and exchange items)
    d) <u>Newspapers</u>: 23 titles (2 by airmail)
3. Staff: 2.5 professionals, 2.86 clericals and students. Japanese bibliographer reports to the Director, Harvard-Yenching

Library. Japanese catalogers report to the Catalog Head, Harvard-Yenching Library. The Director reports to the Harvard College Librarian.

III. **Collection Management**
 1. Classification system: H-Y
 2. Shelving of books: separately by language
 3. Public catalog: cards filed separately by language
 4. Book selection: by Japanese bibliographer, recommendations of faculty members.
 5. Acquisitions: 1973-78, 20,116 volumes, including 178 continuations and 1,242 paid periodical subscriptions. 1978-79, 4,088 volumes, including 33 continuations and 417 paid periodical subscriptions. 1979-10/79, 850 volumes, including 5 continuations and 518 paid periodical subscriptions.
 6. Cataloging: 1978-79, Monographs: 3,444 titles including 385 analytical titles (added volumes, 1,962; L.C. cards, 1,849; other libraries' cards, 41; original cataloging, 534; recataloged, 10).
 7. Circulation: Open hours: M - F, 9 am - 10 pm; Sa, 9 am - 5 pm.
    Sample circulation figures: 1 July to 9 November 1979
    <u>Total</u>: 3,365 items in 3,601 volumes, including interlibrary loans. Subjects in percentages:

Humanities	2,744 items	81%
History, 619		
Art, 412		
Religion, 313		
Social Sciences	584 items	17%
Sciences	36 items	1%
Photoduplication provided		20 items

    <u>Interlibrary loans</u> in 1979 total 1,248 volumes, 10 percent of total Japanese circulation. Loans were made to 150 persons representing 44 institutions, including 32 libraries in New England, 5 elsewhere in the United States, 7 in foreign countries. Furthermore, 69 volumes were sent to 18 institutions free of charge. Visitors are charged for borrowing privileges (use in the library is free). Borrowing fees for Japanese publications are waived for the duration of the Japan-U.S. Friendship Commission grant.
 8. Financing: for Japanese acquisitions, the Harvard-Yenching Institute Fund is the major and consistent source. Of the Library's 1965 to 1979 total budget of $5,776,271, personnel costs represented $3,976,887 and acquisitions $1,465,913. Of the latter, 35 percent was expended on Chinese books, 44 percent on Japanese, 16 percent on Korean, and 5 percent on western publications.
    a) <u>Book budget</u>: 1978-79 (amounts allocated and sources change yearly)

U.S. government agencies	$42,793.96
Foundations	36,167.13
Duplicate sales	350.00
Total	$79,311.09

Funds include monographs and periodical subscriptions. Gifts and exchanges, both monographs and periodicals, are received in great numbers every year. A book sale of duplicate copies, etc., is held once or twice a year, which brings in some additional funds, though these are minimal; the main purpose is to keep duplicate copies in use.

Average price per monograph volume 1978-9	$22.86
Average price per periodical subscription	$23.76

b) <u>Salaries</u>: (1978-79, excluding benefits)

2.5 professional	$44,370
2.86 clerical/students	24,317
Total	$68,687

c) <u>Other expenses</u>: Binding costs are met by university's faculty of arts and sciences budget. Travel expenses provided vary; in 1979-80 no budget for travel was included. Funds are appropriated by the Harvard College Library, of which the Harvard-Yenching Library is now a part.

Harvard-Yenching Library   Nov. 1979, Revised Jan. 1980

The Japanese collection had its beginnings in 1914 as a gift of books made by two Japanese professors who had come to Harvard to study, namely Hattori Unokichi, a sinologist, and Anesaki Masaharu, a buddhologist. It was added to during the years that followed, but was not organized into a collection until Dr. Ch'ui Kaiming was appointed librarian in 1927. In 1928 the Harvard-Yenching Institute was created as an independent corporation under Massachusetts law, and the University assigned five rooms to the Library, with a large reading room and stacks in Boylston Hall, where it remained until its relocation in 1958 to its present site at 2 Divinity Avenue. When Dr. Elisseeff was made Director of the Institute in 1935, the Library had 7,803 Japanese language volumes (see table showing the annual growth, by languages, of the Institute Library's collection from 1927-55, p. 75 of Dr. Elisseeff's article in the Harvard Library Bulletin v. 10, no.1, 1956).

In 1948 the Library acquired the Petzold Buddhist Library, consisting of some 6,500 volumes. Dr. Petzold resided in Japan for many years, studying and practicing Mahayana Buddhism, especially the doctrines of the Tendai sect. His library contained about 200 manuscripts from the 13th and 14th centuries, as well as books printed during the Tokugawa period. Most of these books were incorporated into the general collection, being cataloged under the classification of Buddhism along with representative sets of tripitaka in Tibetan, with Chinese translation collated by Japanese scholars.

In 1955, the Japanese collection numbered 51,133 volumes, or 18 percent of the Institute Library's total holdings. The annual growth of the Japanese collection over the twenty-nine years, 1927-55, averaged 1,705 volumes, while during the last ten years of this period, 1946-55, the average growth was 3,585 volumes per year. In the twenty-four years since 1956, the yearly growth rate has been 4,336 volumes. This steady growth has resulted in a well rounded collection, especially strong in areas of Buddhism, Japanese language and literature, and history. It includes over 9,000 Japanese works on China, a notable collection divided among the various classifications. Its general excellence is further emphasized by the careful and systematic organization of the catalog, which features many analytical entries on titles in collected works. In using the catalog one is aware of the pioneering leadership of Dr. Ch'ui Kaiming in building and servicing this great collection and feels that the tradition he began is still alive in the Library today.

The major task for the second librarian, Dr. Eugene Wu, in his fifteen years with the Library, 1965-80, has been to participate in the fundraising necessary to properly maintain this excellent collection. The budget total for the past fifteen years amounted $5,776,271, of which 69 percent was spent on personnel, 22 percent on acquisitions, and 9 percent on office expenses. Of the acquisitions total during the same period—$1,465,913—35 percent went toward Chinese materials, 44 percent for Japanese, 16 percent for Korean, and 5 percent for Western language materials.

There are two special libraries on the Harvard campus with which the Institute Library cooperates in collecting books. One is the Rubel Asiatic Research collection, housed in the Fogg Art Museum, and the other is the Japanese collection in the Foreign and International Law Library of the Harvard Law School. The Rubel collection is part of the Harvard Fine Arts Library and collects mostly sets of illustrated art books in Chinese, Japanese, and Korean, as well as Western language books on these areas. The approximate budget is $4,000 for all areas, and the collection totals about 11,000 volumes, half of which are Japanese. Over the years a good number of gifts have been received from those countries represented in the collection. The policy of collecting art books for the Rubel collection and the Harvard-Yenching Library has been to divide responsibility between the two, the former specializing in illustrated books and latter in art reviews and art histories.

The other special collection of Japanese books, these pertaining to the law, and numbering about 13,000 volumes, is located in the basement of the Law School Library and is under the supervision of the Foreign and International Law Library. It is used mainly by scholars registered under the East Asian Legal Studies Program, which is directed by Professor Jerome A. Cohen, assisted by visiting Japanese and Chinese legal scholars. It has 7,482 titles and subscribes to 62 reviews, while the Institute library has 1,427 titles under the classification of law. However, the most interesting and valuable part of this law collection is the old documents ranging in date from the 1150's to 1900's. About half of the materials were cataloged and listed by

James Kanda in 1972. (re: Preliminary list of Japanese documents preserved in the Harvard Law School Library, 1972.) The author explains the nature of Japanese feudal law and the transition into the Meiji era in the preface, and then lists each item with short annotations.

When all the known Japanese materials on the campus are added together, the aggregate number of holdings in the Harvard University libraries comes to about 180,000 volumes with less than 1,000 items uncataloged. Once or twice a year a book sale is held by the Harvard-Yenching Library to keep the shelves cleared of unneeded duplicates.

Bibliography

Eliss'eef, Serge. 1954. Japanese collected works and series in the Chinese-Japanese Library at Harvard University. Cambridge, Massachusetts: Harvard-Yenching Institute. (Supplements: Japanese new series in 1961-62, etc.)

Harvard-Yenching Institute. Harvard Alumni Bulletin (December 22, 1933), 360-62.

Kanda, James. 1972. Preliminary report on Japanese documents preserved in the Harvard Law School Library. Mimeographed.

Publications

Current Japanese Language Serials in the Social Sciences and Humanities. Harvard-Yenching Library Occasional Reference Notes, no. 10, 1979. 76p.

Harvard-Yenching Institute: Purposes and Programs, 1928-1968. 1968. 10p.

Law Reviews currently acquired: Japan. 1979. (Typewritten 3 sheets, lists 62 titles.)

User's Guide to the Harvard Law School Library. Guide to the Harvard Libraries, no. 6, 1979. 25p.

UNIVERSITY OF HAWAII

Asian Collection

University of Hawaii, Asian Collection
Established in 1925
2550 The Mall, Honolulu, Hawaii 96822

I. Background
Faculty: 87, including visiting professors
Enrollment: figures not available

II. Organization
1. Location: Fourth and fifth floors of the Hamilton Library
2. Holdings: 1980

   a) Monographs:

Cataloged volumes	66,381
Partly cataloged volumes	12,412
includes 7,336 items of the Kajiyama collection and 4,024 volumes in DC classification	
Total holdings	78,793

   In addition the Okinawa Collection is housed in the East Asia stacks and is available for use through a bibliography compiled by the collection's contributor, Professor Shunzō Sakamaki. (See Ryukyu: a bibliographical guide to Okinawan studies, Honolulu: University of Hawaii Press, 1963.)

   Major subject distribution in percentages:
   Hist. = 28%   Lang. & Lit.= 29%   Soc. Sci. = 24%

L.C. Classification	Titles
General works, Bibliography	839
Philosophy	531
Religion	2,314
History	5,347
Japanese History, 4,174	
Geography	1,036
Social Science, Economics	2,862
Sociology	753
Political Science	971
Law	324
Education	585
Music	128
Fine Arts (including 456 DC titles)	588
Language & Literature	6,603
Japanese Language, 981	
Japanese Literature, 4,737	
Science & Technology	159
Military Science	81
Total	23,121

b) Microfilm: 6,810 reels
  c) Periodicals: current subscriptions, 367 titles
  d) Newspapers: Japan Times and Japan Economic Journal by air.
3. Staff: 4.5 professionals, 1.5 clericals, .5 student help. Japanese Section Head reports to the head of the Asian Collection, who reports to the Director of University Libraries.

III. Collection Management
1. Classification system: L.C., changing from D.C.
2. Shelving of books: languages are intershelved
3. Public catalogs: 1) combined catalog of Chinese, Japanese, and Korean language books; 2) combined catalog of Western language books on East Asia, South and Southeast Asia, as well as books published in the vernacular languages of South and Southeast Asia.
4. Book selection: Professional specialist selects books in the vernacular; the Head of Technical Services selects Western language books.
5. Acquisitions: (including Western language materials) 1976-78, 6,816 titles in 8,742 volumes (2 years); 1978-79, 634 titles in 933 volumes.
6. Cataloging: 1975-78, 6,788 volumes (3 years); 1978-79, 2,466 titles and 362 volumes added (L.C. cards for 856 titles; adjusted L.C. cards, 38 titles; original cataloging, 1,210 titles).
7. Circulation: Open hours: M - Th, 7 am - 10 pm; F, 7 am - 5 pm; Sa, 9 am - 5 pm; Su, 1 pm - 10 pm.
    Sample circulation figures: 1979 circulation for the Asia Library, 24,977 volumes. April 1979 sample of Asia Library users: 1,965 students, 394 faculty and staff, 311 visitors. University of Hawaii Library's computerized circulation system does not generate separate records of the use of Japanese books.
8. Financing:
    a) Book budget: The University of Hawaii allotments are used for materials relating to Japan in Western languages as well as in Japanese. The special funds listed here have been used to purchase Japanese language materials only.

1978-79	
University Library, monographs	$19,855
(Balance brought forward, $285)	
University Library, periodicals	20,500
Special funds	7,085
Total	$47,440
1979-80	
University Library, monographs	$26,795
(Balance brought forward, $5,265)	
University Library, periodicals	20,240
Special funds	2,800
Total	$49,835

b) <u>Salaries</u>: 2.5 professionals, 1.5 clericals, .5 student, total excluding benefits, $59,731. Professionals may take one course tuition free, up to 3 hours a week without making up missed work time.

c) <u>Other expenses</u>: Occasional acquisition list, 210 copies, paid by University Library. Travel expenses are funded by various sources, such as area studies centers, or personally paid.

University of Hawaii   October, 1979, Revised Aug. 1980

The Asian Collection of the University of Hawaii was started in the 1930's with the founding of the Univesity's Oriental Institute. At first limited to Chinese and Japanese language books, with a few in Korean, the scope of the Oriental Library was increased to cover a large Asian region in 1961, when its collection was transferred to the jurisdiction of the new East-West Center, a Federally funded agency located at the University of Hawaii.

In the fall of 1970, the East-West Center was reorganized, and responsibility for its Asia Library was returned to the University. The Asian Library assumed its present name at this time, and underwent several other changes, among them the reduction in scope of its South Asia collection. Today the Asian Collection is housed on the 4th and 5th floors of the Hamilton Library and includes materials in the humanities and social sciences on East, South and Southeast Asia in both Asian and Western languages.

The head of the collection reports to the Director of the University Library, and is in charge of public services, an area divided among professional specialists representing China, Japan, Korea, South and Southeast Asia. These specialists select and order books in the vernacular languages, while the head of technical services is entitled to draw from each area's allocation to purchase books in English.

There is no stated policy concerning the division of the budget for books in the vernacular and in English. There seems to be no coordination of the purchasing of books within the area, e.g. Japan, either in the vernacular or in English. As for books in English, both the University Library and the Asia Library may purchase those on Asia, including Japan.

There are two sets of catalogs in the library's reading room, both containing author-title subject cards in alphabetical order. One covers books in Chinese, Japanese and Korean; the other covers South and Southeast Asian materials, as well as English books on all areas. Books are shelved in two sections following the catalog arrangement. There is a single shelf list, however, in which entries in all languages are interfiled. Serial checklists are located near the catalogs.

Because of the unique geographical and cultural position of Hawaii in relation to Asia, an attempt has been made to keep the area collections equally balanced. Nevertheless, the Japanese collection has increased through outside funding and generous gifts of books, and now consists of some 66,000 cataloged and 17,000 precataloged volumes. The latter group contains special collections, such as one on Okinawa, called the Sakamaki collection for the bibliography published by Prof. Sakamaki. Another, the Kajiyama collection, in addition to books of his authorship, contains 7,000 volumes on Korea, the South Pacific area, Latin America, Manchuria, North China, etc. A bibliography on Korea is being published. (see list of publications)

A qualitative analysis of the Japanese collection is being conducted by the staff by comparing their holdings against subject bibliographies.

Bibliography

East-West Center. 1967. Catalog of the Glen Shaw Collection at the East-West Center Library. Honolulu: East-West Center Library.

Matsuda, Mitsugu. 1968. The Japanese in Hawaii 1868-1967: a bibliography of the first hundred years. Honolulu: University of Hawaii Social Science Research Institute.

Matsui, Masato. 1967. Research resources on Hokkaido, Sakhalin and the Kuriles at the East-West Center Library. Honolulu: East-West Center.

Sakamaki, Shunzo. 1963. Ryukyu: a bibliographical guide to Okinawan studies. Honolulu: University of Hawaii Press.

Sakamaki, Shunzo. 1965. Ryukyuan research resources at the University of Hawaii. Honolulu: University of Hawaii Social Science Research Institute.

Song, Minako, and Masato Matsui. 1980. Japanese sources on Korea in Hawaii. Honolulu: University of Hawaii Center for Korean Studies.

Lists

Books on Japanese literature cataloged since Sept. 1978.

Hawai ni oite shuppansareta Nihongo tosho: Hawai Daigaku Ajia Toshokan shozō

List of Nan'yo shiryo (South Seas materials) published by Nan'yo Keizai Kenkyujo (Institute of South Seas Economic Studies) Tokyo, 1941-44. (All materials uncataloged. This list is classified by area and country. Each item has a temporary shelf number. 236 titles.)

List of the South Manchurian Railway Company publications in the Asia Collection, University of Hawaii Library. (All materials uncataloged. Each item has a temporary shelf number. 213 titles)

Kajiyama Toshiyuki-shi zōsho kizō mokuroku.

THE HOOVER INSTITUTION

East Asian Collection

The Hoover Institution, East Asian Collection
Established in 1945
Stanford, California 94305

I. Background
Faculty: 25
Graduate students: 340 EA
Undergraduates: 875 EA

II. Organization
1. Location: Lou Henry Hoover Building
2. Holdings: 1979
    Monographs: 93,611 cataloged volumes (representing 53,694 titles) plus 7,500 uncataloged miscellaneous volumes (including about 2,000 current publications) plus 487 volumes in the Fine Arts Library; total: 101,598 volumes.

    Major subject distribution in percentages:
    Hist. = 21%   Lang. & Lit.= 15%   Soc. Sci. = 48%

NDC plus L.C. Classification	Titles
General works, Bibliography	1,507
Philosophy	1,525
Religion	1,185
History, Geography	11,230
Japan, 5,835	
Social Science, Economics	13,422
Sociology	3,024
Political Science	5,624
Law	2,157
Education	1,706
Music	54
Fine Arts (in Fine Arts Library)	433
Language & Literature	8,297
Japanese Language, 770	
Japanese Literature, 6,426	
Science & Technology	2,591
Military Science	939
Total	53,694

    b) Microfilm: 533 titles (est.) on 3,872 reels
    c) Periodicals: 290 titles (current subscriptions)
    d) Newspapers: 11 current titles
    e) Document files: 300 items in manuscripts, rare pamphlets, etc.

3. Staff: 3 professionals, 2.5 paraprofessionals, 4 combined Chinese-Japanese, .75 student help. The Japanese Section head reports to the head of the East Asian Collection, who reports to the Director of the Hoover Institution Library.

III. Collection Management
1. Classification system: Nippon Decimal, changing to L.C.
2. Shelving of books: separately by language
3. Public catalog: cards filed separately by language
4. Book selection: By Deputy Curator in charge of the Japanese collection, and recommendations of professors. To coordinate the selection and purchase of expensive items and/or important but little-used items, a joint project with the East Asiatic Library of the University of California at Berkeley has been organized. The members meet once a month. (See the brief report supra, p. 17)
5. Acquisitions: 1973-77, monographs, 14,217 volumes; 1977-78, monographs, 3,821 volumes; 1979-80, monographs, 2,520 volumes (193 continuations), periodical titles, 290 volumes.
6. Cataloging: 1977-78, cataloged 1,755 titles (1,126 by L.C. cards, 629 by original cataloging), added 304 volumes, recataloged 44.
7. Circulation: Open hours: M - F, 8 am - 5 pm; Sa, 9 am - 1 pm.
   Sample circulation figures: (September - December, 1978)
   includes both inside and outside users
   Circulation: 1,376 volumes
   Users: Students, 651; faculty/staff, 392; visitors, 222
   Interlibrary loans: 111
   Circulation by subject, 7/27/79 (NDC classification)

	Titles	Volumes
General	14	15
Philosophy	24	34
Religion	25	25
History (General & Japan)	78	84
(Asia)	23	29
(Biographies, descriptions, and travel)	44	44
Social Science (General)	8	8
Political Science	29	40
Law	21	35
Economics	100	119
Finance, Statistics	8	10
Social Science (others)	102	105
Engineering, Industry	14	17
Productive art (including agriculture, economics, commerce, etc.)	65	81
Art	18	18
Language	19	21
Literature	104	118
(L.C.-classified books)	22	23
Totals	718	826

8. Financing:
   a) <u>Book budget</u>: 1974-1980
   University Library $57,781
   (includes subscriptions)
   Outside funds   5,000
   Total $62,781

b) <u>Salaries:</u> 1978-79 total, $111,070
c) <u>Other expenses:</u> Binding costs paid by Hoover Institution. Professionals are eligible for travel expenses.

The Hoover Institution   August, 1979, Rev. Aug. 1980

There are three main subject areas for collecting books on contemporary China and Japan, established in 1945 by Dr. Harold H. Fisher, then Director of the Hoover Institution, and founder of the collection. They are as follows:

War: The collection would concentrate on the causes and results of war rather than military operations.

Revolution: The collection would deal with all types of revolutionary movements.

Peace: The collection would encompass the whole field of international relations—political, economic, and cultural—and the organization of peace.[1]

In 1958, Professor Nobutake Ike surveyed the Japanese collection. He stated in the General Remarks of his survey report (p. 7):[2]

"The Japanese collection has had an explicitly defined focus in terms of chronological coverage and subject matter. The bulk of the collection pertains to modern and recent history and social sciences, with emphasis on political institutions and movements."

The focus of coverage referred to by Professor Ike includes the period 1914-1945 and such subjects as the right and left-wing political movements, the labor and tenant movements, and so on.

At the time of this first survey the collection held 30,000 volumes of monographs, 1,000 periodical titles, and 300 newspapers rich in material on left-wing as well as ultra-nationalist movements. In addition, the Stanford University Library transferred to Hoover 3,000 volumes of monographs on history and literature, making this library the sole Japanese language collection on the campus. Materials on foreign relations were supported not only by specific books on the subject, but also by descriptive studies of various Asian countries, especially China from World War I through World War II.

Ten years after Professor Ike's report was published the East Asia Colletion was moved from the Hoover Tower to the newly built Lou Henry Hoover Building. The new building is located next to the Tower and houses the collection and offices for international affairs and area studies. The role of the East Asia Collection in Hoover has changed and it now serves as the resource center for teaching and research pertaining to East Asian countries.

The 1958 survey was updated in 1971 by John T. Ma[3], then curator of the East Asia Collection, who followed the same format as the first report, adding titles of subsequent acquisitions.

The present survey shows the predominance of the social sciences, which comprise 55 percent of the total holdings of 54,602 titles in 93,611 volumes. A great number of pamphlets from 10 to 100 pages long in big sets and series are analyzed and cataloged fully so that the titles are readily accessible for research.

Regarding the effort made in recent years to diversify this collection, the current Japanese curator has said, "the holdings in the humanities have increased markedly in the last two decades, reflecting the needs and requirements of Stanford faculty and students who comprise the majority of the collection's users." It is also noted that certain difficulties in acquisition and funding have restricted the continued development of the special social science materials which were the original emphasis of the collection. This is regrettable, since this social science collection, while comparatively small, is unique in the world and of very high quality. The question naturally arises as to what extent this collection will be able to continue its former specialization.

There seems to be a general agreement among those familiar with the collection as to its great value, suggesting that every possible means, including special funding, should be sought to continue its development. (See page 17, "Joint Project of University of California-Berkeley and Hoover Institutions.")

Notes

1. East Asian Collection. Hoover Institution Library Handbook 1978.

2. Nobutake Ike, The Hoover Institution Collection on Japan, Stanford University Collection Survey No. 3, 1958.

3. John T. Ma, East Asia: a survey of holdings at the Hoover Institution on War, Revolution, and Peace (Stanford, California: Hoover Institution, Stanford University, 1971) pp. 17-24.

UNIVERSITY OF ILLINOIS
at Urbana-Champaign

Far Eastern Library

University of Illinois at Urbana-Champaign, Far Eastern Library
Established in 1965
Urbana, Illinois 61801

I. Background
Faculty: 11; visiting professors, 2
Graduate students: 51 (Ph.D. candidates, 3) EA
Undergraduates: 340 EA

II. Organization
1. Location: Third floor of the University Library
2. Holdings:
    a) <u>Monographs</u>: About 32,000 cataloged volumes (representing 15,250 titles); about 3,000 uncataloged books.

    Major subject distribution in percentages:
    Hist. = 26%   Lang. & Lit.= 30%   Soc. Sci. = 25%

L.C. Classification	Titles
General works, Bibliography	716
Philosophy	332
Religion (Buddhism, 445)	764
History	3,550
Japanese History, 2,718	
Geography	340
Social Science, Economics, Sociology	2,567
Political Science	474
Law	502
Education	238
Music	42
Fine Arts	693
Language & Literature	4,611
Japanese Language, 873	
Japanese Literature, 3,175	
Science & Technology	343
Military Science	78
Total	15,250

    b) <u>Microfilm</u>: 116 titles on 295 reels
    c) <u>Periodical subscriptions</u>: 356 titles
    d) <u>Newspaper</u>: 1, by airmail
3. Staff: 2 professionals, 1 paraprofessional, .75 student. The Japanese section bibliograher supervises the general reference and users' services; the Japanese section cataloger supervises the cataloging of Japanese, Chinese and Korean materials. Both report to the Head of the Far Eastern Library, which is under the Technical Services Department.

III. Collection Management
1. Classification system: L.C.
2. Shelving of books: separately by language
3. Public catalog: cards in the author-title catalogs are separated by

    language, but combined in the subject catalog
  4. Book selection: by Japanese bibliographer, and recommendations of professors.
  5. Acquisitions: Monographs: 1973-77, 3,725 volumes; 1977-78, 750 volumes; 1978-79, 1,331 volumes.
  6. Cataloging: 1978-79, 474 monographs (by L.C. cards, 80%; original cataloging, 15%) and 288 added volumes.
  7. Circulation: Open hours: M - F, 8 am - 5 pm.
    Sample circulation figures: (1978-79)
      8,647 items for all Asian languages, about half of which is Japanese books. Total of 4,350 volumes: 3,350 by students; 500 by faculty/staff; 500 by others.
  8. Financing:
    a) <u>Book budget</u>: 1978-79

	University Library allocation	
	Monographs	$20,000
	Subscriptions (est.)	12,000
	Outside funds	<u>10,000</u>
	Total	$42,000

    Average price per volume, $22.50; per subscription, $33.70.

    b) <u>Salaries</u>: 1978-79 Total, $40,000 plus student help.

University of Illinois at Urbana-Champaign   July, 1979, Rev. 1980

  The Asian Library, a department within the Technical Services Department, consists of two administrative units—East Asian, South and West Asian—and three collections: East, South, and West Asia. The reading room and work area of the Library are located on third floor with direct access to the Asian bookstacks and adjacent to the Latin American and African Studies library offices.

  Dr. Sheh Wong is the East Asian and Asian Librarian. A Japanese bibliographer handles Japanese acquisitions and reference, and coordinates Reader's Services for the Asian Library. A Japanese cataloger does the Japanese cataloging and coordinates Technical Services for the Asian Library. As is the case for most Asian Libraries, the staff's work often overlaps. These three professionals have faculty status, entitling them to approximately 10 hours of research time per week and sabbatical leave.

  The East Asian Division's public catalog consists of separate Chinese, Japanese, Korean and Western languages author-title catalogs, and a combined subject catalog. The subject catalog is incomplete due to a large backlog of cards that need to be typed and filed. Most of the large monographic sets have been analyzed and filed in the author-title catalogs.

INDIANA UNIVERSITY

East Asian Collection

Indiana University, East Asian Collection
Established in 1960
Bloomington, Indiana 47401

I. Background
Faculty: 9
Enrollment: figures not available

II. Organization
1. Location: Indiana University Libraries, East Tower, 8th floor
2. Holdings:
    a) <u>Monographs:</u> 23,290 volumes (representing 8,957 titles), plus 500 volumes of uncataloged current imprints, plus 498 volumes in the Fine Arts Library. Total volumes: 24,288.

    Major subject distribution in percentages:
    Hist. = 28%   Lang. & Lit.= 38%   Soc. Sci. = 12%

L.C. Classification	Titles
General works, Bibliography	554
Philosophy	235
Religion	530
History	2,208
Japanese History, 1,290	
Geography, etc.	271
Social Science, Economics, Sociology	688
Political Science, Law	260
Education	120
Music	60
Fine Arts (498 vols. in Fine Arts Lib.)	283
Language & Literature	3,388
Japanese Language, 498	
Japanese Literature, 2,410	
Science & Technology	360
Total	8,957

    b) <u>Microfilm:</u> 381 reels
    c) <u>Periodical subscriptions:</u> 107 titles
    d) <u>Newspaper subscriptions:</u> 2 titles
3. Staff: .5 professional, .5 student assistant. Cataloging is done by the Catalog department. The specialist bibliographer reports to the Assistant Librarian for collection development.

III. Collection Management
1. Classification system: L.C.
2. Shelving of books: books and bound periodicals shelved separately from the Library's general collection; current periodicals kept in general library's reading room.
3. Public catalog: cards interfiled regardless of languages in the General Library's public catalog; a separate shelf list, and a combined Chinese and Japanese author/title catalog are kept near the collection.

4. Book selection: by area specialist bibliographer and recommendations of professors.
5. Acquisitions: 1975-78, Monographs, 3,870 volumes; Periodicals, 104 titles. 1978-79, Monographs, 556 volumes; Periodicals, 107 (69 paid, 38 gifts); Newspapers, 2 titles.
6. Cataloging: 1978-79, Monographs, 220 titles in 541 volumes (L.C. cards 64%, original cataloging, 36%); added bound volumes, 183.
7. Circulation: Open Hours: 8:30 am - 12 midnight, daily.
   Circulation figures not available.
8. Financing: 1979-80
   a) <u>Book budget:</u>

University Library, for Japanese books	$7,342
University Library, for subscriptions	2,800
(1/3 of $8,400 EA subscription fund)	
Outside funds	12,000
Total	$22,142

   Average price per monograph (including items acquired by exchange) = $13.20; average price per Japanese periodical subscription = $40.60.

   b) <u>Salaries:</u> Total (est.) $13,500
   c) <u>Other expenses:</u> Acquisition list for campus circulation paid by general library; binding paid by general library; travel allocated by General Library Travel Committee, for transportation, no perdiem.

Indiana University   August, 1979

The East Asian Collection consists of about 100,000 volumes of Chinese, Japanese, and Korean language books, and is under the direction of Dr. Shizue Matsuda, one of the area bibliographers of the University Library. The various technical processes of book acquisition, cataloging, and binding of periodicals are done by the appropriate sections of the General Library. Cataloged books and bound periodicals are shelved separately from the rest of the University's Western language collection, but current periodicals are kept in the General Library's periodical reading room.

For the convenience of the users of the East Asian Collection, a separate shelf list arranged by language, and an interfiled author-title catalog are maintained adjacent to the collection. All other added entries are available in the public catalog.

In 1979 Dr. Matsuda began a project to compile a union list of current subscriptions to Japanese periodicals in various libraries of the United States. Published as <u>Curent Japanese Serials in the Humanities and Social Sciences Received in American Libraries. June, 1980.</u> Indiana University Library, East Asian Collection, 1980. 337p.

UNIVERSITY OF KANSAS
at Lawrence

East Asian Library

University of Kansas at Lawrence, East Asian Library
Established in 1964
Lawrence, Kansas 66045

I. Background
Faculty: 12 (1975-76)
Enrollment: figures not available

II. Organization
1. Location: Third floor of general library building
2. Holdings:
   a) <u>Monographs:</u> 18,000 cataloged volumes (representing 5,826 titles), plus about 10,000 volumes brief-listed; total about 29,000 volumes.

   Major subject distribution in percentages:
   Hist. = 28%   Lang. & Lit.= 23%   Soc. Sci. = 32%

   L.C. classification, D.C. classification Titles

General works, Bibliography	209
Philosophy	79
Religion	159
History	1,609
Japanese History, 862	
Social Science, Economics, Labor	1,277
Sociology	221
Political Science	206
Law	137
Education	45
Music	7
Fine Arts	361
Language & Literature	1,312
Japanese Lang & Lit, 1,129	
Science, Technology, Military Science	204
Total	5,826

   b) <u>Microfilm:</u> set of Chūō Koron
   c) <u>Periodical subscriptions:</u> about 200 titles
   d) <u>Newspapers:</u> Yomiuri Shimbun (N.Y. edition), 5 other titles in abridged monthly editions
3. Staff: .5 professional, Head East Asian Library—Japan scholar, .5 paraprofessional, .5 student help. The Head reports to the Associate Director for Public Services.

III. Collection Management
1. Classification system: L.C. and D.C. classifications
2. Shelving of books: languages are intershelved
3. Public catalog: languages are interfiled
4. Book selection: East Asian Librarian, reommendations of professors
5. Acquisitions: 1975-78, 3,680 volumes; 1978-79, 1,310 volumes. Serials, continuations, subscriptions: about 225 items.

6. Cataloging: 1978-79, full cataloging by L.C. cards, 440 titles in 1,154 volumes; brief listing, 750 titles in 982 volumes. (The brief-listed books are shelved separately and made available for loan. At present there are about 10,000 volumes in this category.)
7. Circulation: Open Hours: M - F, 8 am - 5 pm
　　Sample circulation figures:
　　　　1978-79, 2,296 Chinese and Japanese items charged
　　　　1978-79, 1,084 brief-listed items used
　　　　1978-79, 3,380 Total items, about half Japanese
8. Financing: 1978-79
　　a) <u>Book budget</u>:

University Lib., Japanese acquisitions	$14,987
University Lib., Japanese subscriptions and continuations (est.)	4,000
Estimated total	$18,987

　　b) <u>Salaries</u>: Total = $16,000
　　c) <u>Other expenses</u>: Binding (University Library allocation) for 700 volumes for East Asian, approximately 350 Japanese periodicals. Travel expenses up to $300 per year for professional staff.

The University of Kansas　　　　　　　　　　　　　　　July, 1979

　　The East Asia library at the time of this report was in the process of moving from the basement to the third floor of the general library building, to an area adjoining the library administration offices. It is expected that the new location will be more accessible to users and more convenient for the staff.

　　The East Asia librarian reports to the general library's associate director for public services. Among his duties is the responsibility, as a bibliographer, to coordinate the library's book selection for all subjects dealing with Asian studies, including those in Western languages. The book budget is allocated to area bibliographers and subject bibliographers, but the East Asia librarian can use funds from subject allocations for books on Asia in general. The financial and other statistics in this particular report are often based upon estimates since the budget and other figures are not drawn up separately for materials on Japan or other East Asian countries.

　　The Asia Library houses the only public card catalog of its books; entries in the various languages are interfiled within a subject and an author-title index. The shelf list entries are also interfiled.

　　The library has an extensive collection of materials on the Japanese Communist Party and related subjects. The materials cover the period to 1975, but have not been kept fully up to date since then. The University Art Library acquired a private collection of the former director of the Freer

Gallery in Washington, D.C., Dr. Harold P. Stern. It consists of 2,000 books and magazines, etc. covering all periods of Japanese art with emphasis on art from the Ukiyoe School of the mid-17th to 19th centuries. Half of the collection is in English and housed at the Art Library. The remaining books are in Japanese and placed in the East Asia Library. They are brief listed and are made available for users.

Reference:

<u>East Asian Studies</u>, by Eugene Carvalho. Lawrence, Kansas, Univ. of Kansas, 1979. 5 typewritten sheets including notes, as follows:

EAST ASIAN STUDIES

by Eugene Carvalho

<u>Purpose</u>

The purpose of the Asian studies collection is to support ongoing and anticipated academic programs at the graduate and postgraduate levels relating to Asian studies in the humanities and social sciences with especial reference to the activities of the Department of East Asian Languages and Cultures and the East Asian Studies program.

Concurrent with emphases on academic programs, the collection's major interests focus on anthropology, art history, geography, history, language and literature, philosophy, religion, political science, sociology, and theater. Encompassing works in Chinese, Japanese, Korean as well as English and other Western languages, East Asian Studies collections provide resource materials needed for a pursuit of independent scholarly investigations. In addition to being both a teaching and a research collection, the library facilitates the development of a higher consciousness on matters Asian both here at the university and in the state of Kansas.

The East Asian Studies collection is a practical, working collection; therefore, the aim is not to collect exhaustively or to provide a "well-rounded collection," but to build extensive strength where academic needs are found.

<u>Collection Guidelines</u>

<u>Languages</u>. Chinese and Japanese materials are collected for the East Asian Library, with English, French and German works on Asia collected primarily for the general Watson Library collection. Korean and other Asian languages are not actively acquired.

<u>Chronological Guidelines</u>. The collection includes materials about all chronological periods.

Geographical Guidelines. The core of Asian studies is East Asian Studies (China, Japan, Korea). South East Asia (Phillipines, Vietnam, Indonesia, etc.) as a whole is studied by itself and in relation to Japan and China.

Treatment of Subject. Reference works on all subjects, including bibliographies and dictionaries in science and technology, are acquired. Publications in both Chinese and Japanese will be selectively added to the East Asian Studies collection on the basis of their contribution to continuing academic programs and to provide an overview of the East Asian area. All scholarly contributions in English on China and Japan will be considered for acquisition.

Type of Material. The collection consists of many types of material, including books and periodicals (monographs, serial publications, encyclopedias, dictionaries, gazetteers, handbooks and collected works), atlases and maps, government documents, pictures and ephemera (including drawings, art prints, and photographs), microfilms, newspapers, pamphlets and propaganda materials (including publications by foreign-language presses of Asian communist countires).

Date of Publication. Both current and retrospective works will be acquired, but the emphasis is on current publications. No preference will be given to editions over reprints, microforms, xeroxed copies, etc.

Other Resources. The Center for Research Libraries holds a limited number of Asian newspapers and serials, as well as some Japanese archives in microforms. As a rule, the materials known to be held in the Center for Research Libraries will not be purchased for the KU library. Sixteenth to eighteenth century accounts of Asia (travelers' reports and Jesuit relations) as well as some rare books and manuscripts in Chinese and Japanese are available in the Department of Special Collections. Travelers' reports are actively collected by the department.

Other Considerations. While duplicate purchase is consciously avoided, translated works into English of books already in the Libraries in original languages are acquired on a selective basis. Materials in Western languages on Asia are located in the main stacks, reference and Art Library collections. Vernacular materials in Chinese, Japanese and Korean on all subjects are located in the East Asian Library. English publications from Asian countries on science are sent directly to the Science Library.

Levels of Collecting Intensity by Subject Subdivision. Letters within parentheses indicate the level of the present collection; letters without parentheses indicate the desired level in the light of clientele and programs served. Key: A. Minimal; B. Basic; C. Study; D. Research; E. Comprehensive; F. Exhaustive.

	Collecting Level	
Anthropology: social anthropology, ethnology, archaeology and folklore	(B)	C
Art and Architecture: fine arts, crafts, religious and traditional architecture of historical and artistic value	(C)	D
Business and economics: historical treatment, statistical works	(A)	B
Education	(A)	A
Geography: local histories, descriptions and travel accounts	(B)	C
History: China (before Ming dynasty)	(C)	D
(Ming & Ching dynasties)	(D)	D
(Republican to present)	(C)	D
History: Japan (pre-Meiji)	(C)	D
(Meiji to present)	(C)	D
History: Korea (general)	(A)	B
Language and literature:		
Chinese & Japanese linguistics	(B)	C
Chinese & Japanese literature	(C)	C
Other Asian literature in Western lanugages	(A)	A
Philosophy	(B)	C
Political science & government: including Japanese & Chinese government documents	(B)	C
Religion	(B)	C
Sociology	(B)	C
Theater: traditional theater and dance of China, Japan, and Korea	(B)	C

LIBRARY OF CONGRESS

Japanese Section

Library of Congress, Japanese Section
Established in 1896
Washington, D.C. 20540

I. Background

As one of the three national libraries of the United States, the Library of Congress has the largest Japanese collection in the country, over 600,000 volumes of Japanese books representing more than 500,000 titles. Administration is through three separate departments: 1) Research Services: Area Studies - Asia - Japanese section; 2) Processing Services: Shared Cataloging Division - Japanese Language Section, Subject Cataloging Division - Asian Materials Section, and Serials Record Division - Foreign Languages Section; 3) Law Library: Far Eastern Law Division. Altogether 36 staff members are involved with the Japanese Collection.

II. Organization

1. Location: Room 1014 in the John Adams Building (former Thomas Jefferson Building or Annex)
2. Holdings: 1979

    a) Monographs and bound volumes of periodicals in volumes and titles (rough estimate):

L.C. classified/cataloged (since 1958)	200,000 vols.
NDC classified/cataloged (up to 1958)	50,000 vols.
Preliminary cataloged	10,000 vols.
Total cataloged monographs	260,000 vols.
Total uncataloged items	340,000 vols.
Grand Total	600,000 vols.

    Major subject distribution in percentages:
    Hist. = 15%   Lang. & Lit.= 25%   Soc. Sci. = 34%

    The L.C. Shelf List as of April 1980 contains 195,486 titles accounting for approximately 260,000 cataloged volumes. To this should be added 27,560 cards to be filed, including 6,500 in social sciences, 18,200 in language and literature, and 2,860 in other subjects, making the estimated grand total 223,046 titles.

    Number of Titles, by Classification

	L.C.	NDC	Total
General works	2,007	696	2,703
Philosophy, Psychology, Religion	10,484	1,380	11,864
History & Science of History	24,967	2,664	27,631
Japanese History (DS 800), 15,190			
Geography, Anthropology	5,620	344	5,964
Social Sciences, Economics	33,810	4,752	38,562

Political Science	4,450	1,510	5,960
Law	18,036		18,036
Education	6,112	200	6,312
Music			
Fine Arts	8,480	872	9,352
Language & Literature	36,078	2,192	38,270
Japanese Language, 2,335			
Japanese Literature, 16,247			
Science & Technology	21,249	2,837	24,086
Military Science	1,890	340	2,230
Bibliography	3,420	1,096	4,516
Totals	176,603 +	18,883	= 195,486

b) <u>Microfilms</u>: Monograph titles, 1,227; periodical titles, 404; number of reels not available.

c) <u>Serials</u>: 14,823 titles listed in cardex including about 5,000 current titles of which 1,076 titles are by purchase. There is a separate file of pre-1958 serial holdings in about 15 card boxes. Some of these titles have been incorporated in the cardex, while others remain untouched. The number of titles in this file is not included in the total figure.

3. Staff:

Research Services - Japanese Section (5 professionals, 4 clericals)	9
Shared Cataloging - Japanese Language Section	16
Subject Cataloging - Asian Materials Section	7
Serials Record - Foreign Language Section	1
Law Library (3 professionals)	3
Total staff	36

III. Collection Management

1. Classification system: L.C. (200,000 vols.) and NDC for pre-1958 holdings (50,000 vols.)
2. Shelving of books: separately by language
3. Public catalog: cards are filed separately by language
4. Book selection: some by Japanese Section staff, but mainly by blanket orders
5. Acquisitions: including books and periodicals obtained through purchase, gifts, and exchange.
    1977-78   17,547 vols.
    1978-79   15,467 vols., including
        12,553 titles in 14,081 vols.   (monographs)
        951 titles in 1,274 bound vols. (serials)
        1 title in 112 reels   (microfilm)

    10,000 unneeded or duplicate items were discarded. Books acquired in Tokyo are included in the above figures.

	Titles	Volumes
1978 Purchase	9,599	12,383

	Gifts	1,166	1,721
	Total	10,765	14,104
1979	Purchase	7,501	9,439
	Gifts	715	1,061
	Total	8,216	10,500

6. Cataloging: 1978-79, all original cataloging

	Titles	Volumes
Monographs:	12,553	14,081
Serials, additions:	951	1,274
Microfilm, additions:	1	(reels) 112
Recataloged:	4,488	4,889

a) <u>Printing Master Cards</u>

One of the most important contributions to Japanese collections in the United States is the distribution of printed L.C. cataloging cards. The procedure of compiling the cards originates in the Japanese National Diet Library's (NDL) system of computer-printed cards, which are sent free of charge to the Library of Congress Tokyo office. The yearly total for 1977-78 was 48,306 cards, an average of 947 per week. For 1978-79 it was 38,695 cards, an average of 757 per week. There was a 19.9 percent decrease in 1979, because the NDL was transfering entries in the Nōhon Shūhō to the computer-printed cards. This change to the computerized system will be completed by 1980.

Book orders are selected from these cards, at an average rate of 196 per week for 1977-78 (totaling 9,972 orders), and at an average rate of 157 per week for 1978-79 (totaling 8,011). The 19.7 percent decrease is for the reason given above. Orders originating at the Library of Congress and those from other libraries received by the Library of Congress are also sent to Tokyo for bibliographic searching. The number of these outside order slips was reduced by 75 percent in 1978-79, amounting to 401 titles, compared to 1,639 titles received in 1977-78.

After the books are selected and ordered, they are cataloged with preliminary entries based on NDL cards and sent to the Library of Congress for complete cataloging. In 1978-79, 8,417 entries were verified, 20.5 percent fewer than the 10,540 verified in 1977-78. When NDL cards are not available, the entries are sent to the Library of Congress for original cataloging. There were 200 such entries in 1979. Manuscripts for the master cards from the Library of Congress are sent to Tokyo for photo-set composition. They are proofread and sent back to the

Library of Congress to be printed on cards. During 1978-79, 16,068 cards for monographs and 352 cards for serials, a total of 16,240 cards, were completed.

b) <u>Cards filed:</u> March 1980

Shelf list cards: up to 23,000 cards filed per year
Japanese Union Catalog: up to 53,000 cards filed per year

1) L.C. classification shelf list: 144,260 cards on file
 H section: 6,500 cards ready to be filed
 P section: 18,200 cards ready to be filed
 Mixed: 2,860 cards ready to be classified for filing

2) NDC shelf list for pre-1958 holdings contains over 18,000 titles in 50,000 volumes.

3) MARC DATA cards: 1979
 a. MARC-S data base on perforated 3 x 5 cards, May 1973 to August 1979, representing 2,983 titles, was filed in the L.C. shelf list.
 b. MARC data base for books on Japan in Western languages from August 1977 to the present, a total of about 1,500 titles, was also filed in the L.C. classification shelf list.

c) Japanese Union Catalog: 1978-79

The idea of the union catalog originated in the 1930's, but it was during the last few years that it developed into its present form.

Cards received from various libraries for the Japanese union catalog are arranged alphabetically by main entry and filed. They are not compiled into one card with location stamps. Therefore, the total number of cards indicates the number of cards received, not titles. At present, the catalog includes cards up to the letter "I".

As of July 1, 1979, a total of 675,000 cards (rounded estimate) had been received:
 Main body of interfiled cards (A-I): 320,000*
 Outside cards, alphabetized (A-I):   68,300*
 Outside cards, unalphabetized (mostly
  mixed cards, J-Z)   225,000
 Alphabetized L.C. cards: 36,000
 Unalphabetized L.C. cards: 25,000
  *By February 1, 1980, these figures were 356,910 and 31,000 respectively.

The Library of Congress has other card catalogs for its own holdings; therefore, it has not been necessary to file extra cards for their location.

The target date for finishing the A-I section is July 1, 1980. After the present sections are completed, a procedure for interfiling the unalphabetized outside cards (some 225,000) will be established.

d) Uncataloged materials: 340,000 volumes (est.)
Duplicates, unneeded materials, books related to science and technology, and periodicals are arranged on shelves in the Landover storage building.

In summary, the Japanese section of the Library of Congress has over 200,000 volumes cataloged according to the L.C. classification system, materials acquired since 1958. (See the Library of Congress East Asia catalog, published in 1972.) Pre-1958 holdings are classified according to the Nippon Decimal Classification and total about 50,000 volumes. Approximately 10,000 volumes in the preliminary cataloging process should be added to these two groups.

During a normal fiscal year, between 14,000 and 15,000 volumes of current imprints are received and cataloged, while about 2,000 volumes are recataloged, leaving over 5,000 volumes for full cataloging.

7. Circulation: Open Hours: M - F, 8:30 am - 5 pm; Sa, 8:30 am - 12:30 pm.
Sample circulation figures (Reading room use only):
Monthly book use averages 1,700 volumes.

```
Interlibrary loan and photoduplication requests: 1978-79
      Monograph requests received:             698
      Monograph requests filled (93%):         661
      Serials requests received:             1,600
      Serials requests filled (65%):           862
            Total received:                  2,298
            Total filled (75%):              1,523
```

Reference services: 896 items serviced in February 1980.

8. Financing:
   a) <u>Expenses for Tokyo office</u>: 1979
       1) Administration: A total of ¥25,321,303 ($123,518.55; $1.00 = ¥205), including personnel salaries and benefits for 7.5 staff members. 59.3 percent of this is for NPAC and 16.2 percent for non-NPAC personnel (mostly proofreaders).
       2) Purchase of Japanese books: In 1979, ¥29,007,873.10 ($141,501.82) was expended for 10,500 volumes, an average of ¥2,763 ($13.48) per volume.
       3) Photoset master cards: In 1979, ¥21,368,100 ($104,234.63) was expended for Japanese language

materials, exceeding the $90,000 annual budget.

b) <u>Salaries:</u>
Reference Services, Japanese Section: 5 professionals plus 4 clericals (1978 base pay): $181,673
Processing, Shared Cataloging, Japanese Language Section: 11 professionals plus 5 clericals (1980 base pay): $331,072
Subject Cataloging, Asian Materials Section: 7 professionals (1979 base pay): $173,501
Serials Record, Foreign Language: 1 professional (1979 base pay): $24,703
Law Library, Far Eastern, Japanese: 3 professionals (1979): $63,911

c) <u>Serial subscriptions:</u> 1,076 titles, paid by the Order Department.

d) <u>Probable minimum cost of completing a catalog card:</u> 1979
It is said that the average cost of cataloging a Western language book and processing it for service is about $75.00 at the Library of Congress. In the case of Japanese books the process involves both Japan and the United States; nevertheless, the process up to completing a master catalog card ready for off-set printing costs $53.20. (Marking and shelving books is done in the same way as for other language books; the cost of these cannot be estimated.)

1) Tokyo office, NPAC expenditure: ¥21,231,329 ($103,567.45) for book selection, ordering, purchase, mailing, preliminary cataloging, office space, etc. The computer printout cards used for preliminary cataloging by the Tokyo office are gifts from the National Diet Library to the Library of Congress, so their cost is not included.

2) Printing of Japanese master cards: ¥21,368,100 ($104,234.63) for 16,068 monograph titles and 352 serial titles, an average per title of
$6.38

3) Books purchased: (1978-79) ¥29,007,873.10 ($141,501.82) for 8,216 titles in 10,500 volumes, an average of $17.22 per title and $13.48 per volume. When office expenses are added to the amount for books purchased, the total is $245,069.27, an average per volume of $21.40 and per title of
$29.82

4) Cataloging staff at the Library of Congress: Base pay estimated at $429,276. 31,117 cards were sent to the Tokyo Office for photosetting, making the average cost per card

$17.00

5) Total cost per title (per finished master catalog card):

$53.20

Library of Congress   April, 1980

The pre-war development of the Japanese collection of the Library of Congress has been documented and described in detail by Mr. Andrew Kuroda. (See the article beginning on page 83.) By the end of World War II, there were close to 50,000 volumes; to these were added some 300,000 volumes which had been gathered from several collections by the now defunct Japanese military agencies. About 20,000 new books had been purchased by 1954, bringing to a total of 370,000 the number of volumes added since World War II.

The Tokyo office opened in 1968, by which time the collection of the Japanese section already consisted of about 450,000 volumes. Since then not only has the size of the collection increased to more than 600,000 volumes, but also the size of the office areas and the number of staff members have grown rapidly to meet the challenge of an ever-increasing work load.

The pre-war Orientalia, once housed on Deck F of the main building, now occupies the south half of the first floor of the John Adams Building (formerly called the Annex). The Processing Department assumed the job of cataloging the books after the relocation in 1958, while the Japanese section retained the duties of checklisting the serials.

As part of the Library of Congress, the Japanese section serves as a research library for the legislature and government agencies, as well as an information center on Japan to these organizations. To this end, broad selections of Japanese books are collected, including representative works of popular culture as well as scholarly treatises. And since it is part of the national depository library as well, the section receives Japanese government documents in exchange for their U.S. government counterparts.

The Tokyo office was formed to expedite the National Program for Acquisition and Cataloging (NPAC), which was already in operation in European countries. In conjunction with the Diet Library, the Tokyo office developed a system for sharing information on book selections and cataloging, which has been working efficiently ever since. As part of this information sharing, the Library of Congress makes available to the Diet Library its MARC tapes, which generate a computer printout of the Library of Congress recent acquisitions of books in several languages. Furthermore, the existence of the Tokyo office has brought about deeper understanding and cooperation between the two countires, which are able to exchange ideas and promote goodwill by receiving visiting librarians from the partner country as well as the rest of the world.

During the last several years, the work of producing photoset master cards for Chinese and Korean books has been added to the tasks of the Tokyo office, firmly establishing its role as a leader in cataloging with characters. In 1979, ¥18,904,500 ($92,217.07) was expended on photoset master cards:

	Monographs	Serials
Chinese	8,533	62
Korean	1,991	382
Total	10,524	444

Grand total of 10,968 cards @ ¥1700 per card.

This is only a short outline of the enormous complex which is the Japanese operation of the Library of Congress. The 36 employees (excluding the Tokyo office) comprise about six percent of the 5,700 employees of the Library of Congress (by comparison, the University of Michigan Library has seven Japanese collection staff out of a total of 420, or about two percent). The difference can partly be explained by the fact that the Library of Congress provides printed catalog cards which supply 70-80% of such cards needed by university libraries. The cost of producing each individual card is formidable for the Library of Congress, and of course represents a corresponding saving for the receiving library. A pressing question is whether the Library of Congress can continue to meet the rising cost of producing these cards, or whether the receiving libraries will have to contribute to this cost to keep the level of service at today's high standard.

Bibliography

Beal, Edwin G. 1954. Orientalia: Japan. Library of Congress Quarterly Journal of Current Acquisitions 11:91-94.

Hummel, Arthur W. 1954. The growth of the Orientalia Collections. Library of Congress Quarterly Journal of Current Acquisitions 11:69-87 (pp. 80-81 on Japanese section).

Kim, Hong N. 1979. Library of Congress A30. Scholar's guide to Washington, D.C., East Asian studies. Washington, D.C.:

Smithsonian Institution Press.

Kuroda, Andrew Y. 1970. History of the Japanese collection in the Library of Congress, 1874-1941. In Senda Masao Kyoju koki kinen toshokan shiryō ronshū. Tokyo: Senda Masao Kyoju Koki Kinenkai.

Kuroda, Andrew Y. 1978. The U.S. Library of Congress and its Japanese collection. Paper read at the joint meeting of the Asiatic Society of Japan and the German East Asiatic Society in Tokyo on September 11, 1978.

Publications

Checklist of Archives in the Japanese Ministry of Foreign Affairs, Tokyo, Japan, 1868-1945. Microfilmed for the Library of Congress, 1949-1951. Compiled by Cecil H. Uehara, under the direction of Edwin G. Beal. Photoduplication Service, Library of Congress, 1954. 262 p.

Checklist of microfilm reproduction of selected archives of the Japanese Army, Navy, and other government agencies, 1868-1945. Compiled by John Young. Washington, D.C.: Georgetown University Press, 1959. 144 p.

Guide to Japanese reference books: supplement. (Translation of Nihon no sanko tosho: hoiban.) Translated by Mayumi Taniguchi et al. Library of Congress, 1979. 300 p.

Current Japanese national government publications in the Library of Congress. Forthcoming.

Bibliographic Projects

1. Checklist of Pre-Meiji publications in the Library of Congress on the subject of Japanese mathematics. About 500 titles of an estimated 4,500 entries reviewed (as of 1980) for publication.

2. Japanese local history of about 1,600 titles, edited for future publication.

3. Checklist of Japanese microfilms of about 1,500 titles, arranged by control number, title, and author.

4. South Manchurian Railroad Company materials' microfilming project. There are two publications checklisting items in the Library of Congress:

a) <u>The Research Activities of the South Manchurian Railroad Company, 1907-1945: A History and Bibliography.</u> By John Young. Columbia University, New York East Asian Institute, 1966. 682 p. (Annotated list of 5,011 items.)

b) <u>Kyu shokuminchi kankei kikan kankobutsu sogo mokuroku: Minami Manshu Tetsudo Kabushiki Kaisha hen.</u> (Union catalog of the publications of the former colonies: South Manchurian Railroad Co.) Edited by Ajia Keizai Kenkyujo, 1979. 657 p. Tables. (Contains 10,514 items, including monographs, serials, documents, found in about 50 Japanese and 6 U.S. libraries. Index to be published.)

Some of the items listed in Young's books as holdings of the Library of Congress could not be found at the time the Ajia Keizai Kenkyujo compiled the checklist. There are still times when unlisted titles are found in the Library of Congress, among uncataloged materials. At present, all the literature concerning the South Manchurian Railroad Co., both cataloged and uncataloged, has been gathered together in Deck 8 South (Japanese Books stacks), in order to expedite the microfilming of materials that are in the Library of Congress, but missing in Japan. The work was started in 1979. As the items are filmed, they are recorded on cards and filed under the MOJ (Microfilm Orientalia Japan) control number; about 800 such cards have been filed since the start of the project.

Library of Congress, Law LibraryApril, 1980
Far Eastern Law Division's Japanese Collection

Location: West side of the Main building, 2nd floor. To reach the Japanese collection, one must go through the Law Library reading room and down the hallway where the regional law research section is located. At the end of this hallway of stacks and carrels is the Far Eastern Law Division, headed by Dr. Hsia. Access to the stacks for law books is by way of the office area. Up to 1958, Japanese books for the Law Library were classified according to the NDC, and books acquired after 1958 are arranged roughly in the following way:

		Number of Titles
A	Administrative Law	1,425
C	Constitutional Law	1,241
CM	Commercial Law	1,821
CP	Civil Procedure	709
CR	Criminal Law	1,045
CRP	Criminal Procedure	452
CV	Civil Law	2,028

F	Foreign Law	680
H	Horitsugaku (Jurisprudence)	1,557
I	International Law	396
LH	Legal History	458
R	Rodoho (Labor Law)	1,303
RS	Rombunshu (Festschriften)	305
T	Tokubetsuho (Special Law)	2,497
Z	Zeiho (Tax Law)	1,244
Dictionaries		75
Set collections		800
Total		18,036

Summary of Resources

   Total titles: approximately 18,000

   Total volumes: estimated to be around 60,000, including bound periodicals. NDC classification books have been largely recataloged, with about 1,000 titles remaining to be recataloged.

   Acquisitions: Expended $14,816.67 during 1979 for blanket order to Japan Publications Trading Co. for books.
   Subscription to periodicals is paid for by the Law Library. Currently, 450 periodical titles are received, 50 percent as gifts and by exchange, 50 percent by purchase.

   Cataloging: done by the Japanese section of the Shared Cataloging Division.

   Personnel: 3 professionals (1 in reference and research, 2 in processing and reader service)

   Publications:
   1) "The Tokyo War Crimes Trial," by Sung Yoon Cho. Quarterly Journal of the Library of Congress, Vol. 24, No. 4, October, 1967, pp. 309-318.
   2) Japanese Writings on Communist Chinese Law, 1946-1974: A selected annotated bibliography. Compiled by Sung Yoon Cho. 1977. 223 p. 1,086 entries.
   "Periodical holdings of the Far Eastern Law Division including China, Japan, Korea." To be published.
   "Western language materials on Japanese law in the Far Eastern Law Division"; also on Korean law. To be published.

THE U.S. LIBRARY OF CONGRESS AND ITS JAPANESE COLLECTION

Andrew Y. Kuroda

The Library of Congress was established in 1800 with 152 titles consisting of 740 volumes of books as its collection. One hundred and seventy-eight years and 11 Librarians of Congress later, today the Library is probably the world's largest library. Its resources contain information on virtually every subject known to man and include all forms of preserved thought, from papyrus to microform.

Growing at the rate of one and a half new item every second, or over 7,000 new items every working day, the collection stretch along 350 miles or 563 kilometers of book shelves. In addition to 18 million books, two-thirds of which are in 470 different foreign languages, the Library now has 32 million manuscripts, including the papers of 23 American Presidents, 3 and a half million maps and atlases, and 4 million pieces of music from classical to rock. It also contains 8 million prints and photographs, half a million sound recordings rich in American folklore and music, a quarter of a million reels of motion pictures and 3 million pieces of microforms.

These vast collections are housed in a complex of buildings on Capitol Hill. Across the plaza from the Capitol is the ornate Library of Congress Building, a landmark since 1897. Behind it is the Thomas Jefferson Building, a classically simple annex completed in 1939. The spacious white marble James Madison Memorial Building to the south will open in 1980, making room for the continuing expansion of knowledge.

Probably the first Japanese ever to visit the Library of Congress was Joseph Heco. I said "probably", because I cannot document it. However, since Heco worked as a clerk in the office of Senator William M. Gwin of California from October 1857 to February 1859, it is most likely that Heco visited the Library located at that time in the Capitol building.

The first contact made by the Japanese with the Library of Congress took place in 1860, when the three ambassadors of the first diplomatic mission of Japan visited the Capitol on Wednesday, May 23. They were in Washington to exchange documents of ratification of the Treaty of Commerce between the United States and Japan of 1858. The visit to the Capitol is recorded in the diaries kept by Norimasa Muragaki (Awaji no Kami), Deputy Ambassador, and by Yasushige Tamamushi, an aide to Chief Ambassador Masaoki Shinmi (Buzen no Kami).

The 1860 Mission took back to Japan 160 titles in 218 volumes of

American, mostly government, publications given to members of the party, and 14 titles in 346 volumes purchased during the trip to the United States. No Japanese book was included among the gifts the Ambassadors brought to the United States.

Earlier, when Commodore Matthew Calbraith Perry came to Japan with his fleet to open the door of a reluctant Japan in 1853 and 1854, he took 18 titles of books in 41 volumes among the United States gifts to Japan. He did not, however, include Japanese books in his list of desiderata of gifts from Japan. Later, the United States Consulate General was opened in Shimoda, and Townsend Harris arrived as the first American diplomatic officer in 1856. It is conceivable that some Japanese publications were shipped to the Department of State by Harris. To the best of our knowledge, however, no Japanese books exist now in the Library of Congress with accession dates going back to those days.

It was through the initiative of Ainsworth Rand Spofford, 6th Librarian of Congress, that the channel was established in late 1875 between the governments of the United States and Japan for the purpose of exchanging publications of their respective governments. In 1876 a small number of Japanese books began coming in to the Smithsonian Institution, which served even then as a transmittal agency for exchange shipments. These books formed the earliest accessioned items of the present Japanese Collection in the Library of Congress. Some of the titles are: Nihon sanbutsu shi, by Keisuke Itō, a Monbushō publication of 1873, Rikugunshō jōrei, 1874, Shōgaku tokuhon, 6 vols. 1874, and Heiyō Nihon chiri shōshi, 1875.

In those early years no linguistic and subject expertise was available to the Library of Congress for recommending the purchase of Japanese books. Consequently, the main sources of acquisition were exchange and gift. In October 1905 the Library received as gifts from Crosby Stuart Noyes of Washington his entire collection of Japanese art, which included 12 watercolors, 145 original drawings, 331 wood engravings, 97 lithographs, 658 illustrated books, and 61 other items, representing works produced from the mid-18th century to the 19th century. Mr. Noyes was the publisher and editor-in-chief of the Washington newspaper Evening Star for over 40 years. He travelled frequently and widely. Attracted by Japanese art, first by its impact on European artists he began collecting Japanese art, art objects, and art books in Europe and Japan. In his letter of transmittal to Herbert Putnam, Librarian of Congress, he said:

> "It is the art that taught Whistler his exquisite draughtsmanship and brush work, subtle gradations of tone and dainty color harmonies; the art from which Manet and the French school of impressionists got their inspiration, and that, as Hartmann declares, has influenced the several

lines of work of Whistler, Manet, Degas, Skarbina, the German Secessionists, Puvis de Chavannes, D.W. Tryon, Steinlein and Monet; and he adds "that nearly two-thirds of all painters who have become prominent during the last twenty years have learned in one instance or another from the Japanese."

For Noyes, however, Japanese art did not remain simply as things to be viewed and appreciated. He undertook to study the people who produced it. "The pursuit of this inquiry," said he, "will necessarily lead to a close study of the antecedents of the Japanese; their history, life, manners and customs, industries and arts, and it is believed that this collection will afford the inquirer a considerable amount of information." The gift was accompanied by a 22-page catalog which Noyes commissioned an unidentified Japanese to compile. Included in the collection are "gachō", "gafu", and formats of a similar nature of 119 individual artists such as Beisen, Bunchō, Hiroshige, Hokusai, Kuniyoshi, Utamaro, and others, 54 anonymous individual artists, and 31 title of collected works.

The first serious attempt by the Library to form a Japanese collection was successfully completed when 9,072 volumes of books, carefully selected by Kan-ichi Asakawa of Yale University, were delivered in 1907 and 1908. Asakawa was born in Nihonmatsu, Fukushima prefecture in 1873. After graduating from Tokyo Semmon Gakko, now known as Waseda University, in 1895, he entered Dartmouth College, from which he was graduated in 1899 with a B. Lit. degree. Taking graduate study at Yale University, he obtained his doctorate in 1902 with a dissertation entitled <u>The Early Institutional Life of Japan: A Study in the Reform of 645 A.D.</u> He lectured on the history and civilization of East Asia at Dartmouth College from 1902 to 1905. Before he began to teach at Yale University in the fall of 1907, Asakawa decided to spend one and half years in Japan to collect materials for his research. When Yale University learned of Asakawa's plan, it commissioned him to select and purchase Japanese books, primarily in the field of history for its library. A suggestion was also made to Herbert Putnam, the Librarian of Congress, to take similar advantage of his service. The Librarian invited Asakawa to Washington to talk over the matter and an inspection of the then meager Japanese collection, and he sent a letter to Asakawa to make the Library's request official and in writing. I find that the following passage from the Librarian's letter to Asakawa significant:

> What we desire for the Library of Congress is the beginning of what may ultimately prove a considerable department of Japanese literature. We wish to make this beginning now, taking advantage of your aid, but we do not anticipate immediate practical use of it. We therefore wish to avoid including in it material ephemeral in nature, or merely critical or otherwise secondary material. What

we do wish to acquire so far as the money available for the
purpose will permit, is a carefully selected list in the best
editions of the books fundamental to a knowledge of
Japanese history and institutions; and in addition to these a
selected list of the more important works in Japanese
literature proper.

Asakawa's report of the acquisitions is incorporated in the 1907 <u>Annual Report</u> of the Librarian of Congress. He acquired for the Library such basic sets as the <u>Nihon daizōkyō</u>, <u>Nihon zoku zōkyō</u>, <u>Kokushi taikei</u>, <u>Shiseki shūran</u>, and others. He also purchased works of local history, gazetteers, hand painted and wood-block maps of the Tokugawa period, folklore, literature, and illustrated works by Moronobu and others. Referring to the Buddhist books he purchased for the Library, he said, "It is gratifying to see that about Japanese Buddhism in particular we have secured perhaps as complete a collection of material as can be found in any one library in Japan." Among rare items Asakawa purchased are four works of Buddhist sutras hand copied in the 15th and 16th centuries, and five illustrated scrolls of Shinto cosmogony handwritten in the 16th century. One unfortunate lapse in judgment on the part of Asakawa was to destroy the original Japanese bindings of pre-Meiji works and to rebind the books in the European fashion.

In the conclusion of his report Asakawa modestly implied his belief that the collection he gathered in Japan for the Library of Congress "may be regarded as a foundation of a Japanese library more perfect than can be found anywhere else outside of Japan." His collection, indeed, became a foundation on which the present Japanese Collection of the Library of Congress has come to be the largest outside of Japan.

For the next two decades, however, the eminently scholarly and highly valuable collection that Dr. Asakawa obtained for the Library of Congress lay dormant in the stacks, because no one inside and outside of the Library could exploit it. The situation was a reflection of the general lack of interest in Japanese studies in America at that time. No university in America started its Japanese collection as early as Yale and the Library of Congress. Columbia started its Japanese collection in 1921, Harvard in 1928, and Northwestern in 1933. All other collections now housed in major centers of Japanese studies in American universities started only after World War II. Even at Yale where Dr. Asakawa joined the faculty after he returned from Japan with anticipation of teaching Japanese studies courses, not enough students signed up. Dr. Asakawa was forced to shift his field of speciality to European feudalism. Dr. Putnam accurately assessed the situation when he stated about a proposed Japanese collection in his letter of January 20, 1906 to Asakawa: "We wish to make this beginning now, taking advantage of your aid; but we do not anticipate immediate practical use of it."

During this interim period of 20 years, the chief benefactor of the Japanese Collection was Walter Tennyson Swingle, a noted botanist at the Bureau of Plant Industry of the United States Department of Agriculture from 1891 to 1941. As a botanist specifically interested in improving citrus fruits, he was greatly impressed by the fact that 27 varieties of oranges and their methods of cultivation were described in a treatise of 1178 A.D. entitled Chu lu by a Chinese named Han Yen-chih. He was determined to utilize the wisdom of more than 40 centuries in the culture and use of plants accumulated in Chinese books, records, and traditions. Thus, he became an enthusiastic supporter of enriching the Chinese collection of the Library of Congress. While on an official trip to the Far East in the spring and summer of 1915 on behalf of the United States Department of Agriculture, Swingle obtained in China and Japan nearly 6,000 volumes of Chinese, Japanese, and Korean works. Included were 176 Japanese titles bound in 770 volumes and 9 serial titles. Among them were Senchaku hongan nenbutsu shū and three other 13th century "jōdokyō han," Shaku maka enron, 13th century "Kōya han," Zōjō hōsū, 15th century "Ouchi han," and Shūbun inryaku, 16th century "Ouchi han." He took another trip to the Far East from April 1918 to February 1919 for the Department of Agriculture, and acquired 15,000 Oriental works in 16,200 volumes, including 435 titles in 2,700 volumes of Japanese works.

The Japanese Collection was placed under the administrative control of the Division of Chinese Literature when it was officially created, and Arthur William Hummel was appointed Chief of the Division in 1928. The Division of Chinese Literature changed its name to the Division of Orientalia in 1932, and the Chinese Section and the Japanese Section were created within the Division in 1938. The name of the Division changed to Orientalia Division in 1940.

The Japanese Collection in the Library of Congress turned into, for the first time, an area of growing activity when Dr. Shio Sakanishi was appointed as assistant to the Chief of the Division of Chinese Literature. She was eminently qualified as a "Japanese area specialist," although no such title existed in the Library at that time. Miss Sakanishi, born in Tokyo, studied in Tokyo Women's Christian College, and received her B.A. degree (1925) from Wheaton College, Norton, Massachusetts, and her M.A. (1926), and Ph.D. degrees (1929) from the University of Michigan, Ann Arbor, Michigan. She served one year as Assistant Professor at Hollins College, Hollins College, Virginia, before coming to the Library.

One would be impressed with the Librarian's foresight in creating a position for Miss Sakanishi when one considers the status of Japanese studies in the United States in 1930. At that time Japan was not an area of serious academic interest or research. This was reflected in the fact that among American universities only Yale, Columbia, and Harvard had a Japanese collection in their libraries. Hardly any American was teaching any course related to Japanese studies in an American university. Only a few Japanese like Dr. Kan-ichi Asakawa of Yale, Mr. Ryusaku Tsunoda of Columbia and Mr. Yoshisaburō Kuno of the University of California, Berkeley, in addition to Mr. Kojiro Tomita of the Boston Museum of Fine Arts, were considered to be specialists in various areas of Japanese studies. Asakawa, a specialist in feudalism of Europe and Japan, resented being considered among scholars of Japanese studies, insisting that he did not know much about Japan except for feudalism.

Some of the present American "elder" and senior scholars in Japanese studies were still students in 1930. Dr. Hugh Borton and Dr. Charles B. Fahs, for instance, were in graduate school working for M.A. degrees. Dr. Edwin O. Reischauer was an undergraduate working for his A.B. degree. Dr. John Whitney Hall of Yale University received his A.B. degree in 1939. Most of these "elder scholars" went to Tokyo, Kyoto, or Paris to equip themselves with linguistic proficiency, because of the paucity of language-teaching facilities in American universities. The other Americans who had proficiency in the Japanese language were mostly foreign service officers or missionaries. Among them only a few, like Dr. Karl August Reischauer and Dr. Daniel Clarence Holtom, were scholarly types, but they usually remained at their posts.

The decade of the 1930's, then, was the formative period in the history and development of Japanese studies in the United States. It had also become the most difficult period in the history of United States-Japan relations except for the actual period of armed hostilities. As the relations between the two nations had increasingly worsened, so had the need by America and Americans to have better knowledge of the potential enemy and his country also increased. Yet, actually any dissemination of information on Japan, even purely cultural, if done by Japanese nationals, was increasingly suspected as propaganda. Japanese studies became unpopular. When the war came, therefore, the nation was caught with extremely short supply of persons of linguistic and other expertise needed to prosecute the war. The United States government had to resort to crash programs to produce many thousand "instant experts" on short notice to meet various needs of the emergency. It is by placing Miss Sakanishi's appointment to the Library of Congress in 1930 and her service during the fateful and difficult decade that followed in proper historical perspective, that one gains a deeper sense of appreciation of Dr. Putnam's appointment of Miss Sakanishi to the Library.

With a sense of urgency Miss Sakanishi skillfully organized the large, unprocessed collection of Japanese books in such a way that, even before they were properly cataloged, they might be easily retrieved. She cataloged books, checked in new serial pieces, selected and recommended books and periodical titles for acquisitions. She was anxious not only to fill the gap in the collection created by twenty years of neglect, but also to acquire as many titles as possible of currently available reference works as well as standard scholarly works.

Miss Sakanishi brought back from her two-months acquisition trip to Japan in the fall of 1937 a large number of Japanese works in traditional format. Included among them are nearly 300 works of the so-called "kibyōshi" by such authors as Santō Kyōden, Jippensha Ikku, and Koikawa Harumachi, nearly 200 volumes of haiku works, a number of illustrated story books of the Tokugawa period. When she came to the Library, the Japanese collection numbered about 12,000. When she left, it had almost trebled, numbering about 34,000.

Miss Sakanishi's work in the Library ended abruptly on December 7, 1941. According to her own account, she was invited to a lunch at the home of the former United States Ambassador to Argentina, Robert Woods Bliss and Mrs. Bliss. She heard the radio news about the Pearl Harbor attack at 3:00 p.m. and was taken into custody by Federal agents at about 5:00 p.m. She was one of those marked for detention as "dangerous" enemy aliens throughout the United States mainland and Hawaii when the war broke out, to be exchangeable with Americans held by the Japanese in Japan and Japanese occupied areas.

Although the U.S. Department of Justice advised employers not to drop aliens from their rolls until the Department had reviewed individual cases, many Japanese-Americans (even U.S. citizens) were dismissed from their jobs, particularly on the West Coast. Miss Sakanishi's actual performance of her duties in the Library ended with her detention on December 7, 1941, but she was not summarily dismissed from the staff. Archibald MacLeish, then Librarian of Congress, ruled that it would be unfair to her to take action before her case had been reviewed, and her name remained on the Library's roll until June 18, 1942, the date of her departure on the exchange ship, Gripsholm. Edwin G. Beal, Jr., who had joined the staff in September 1941 and had acted in Miss Sakanishi's place during her detention, became her successor.

The war greatly affected the Library of Congress. First of all, valuable library materials were selected and removed for safe-keeping for the duration in eight localities approved by the War Department. Master Library catalogs which could not be removed from the Library buildings were microfilmed and film was deposited elsewhere for safekeeping.

The collections of the Library were intensively as well as extensively used by many newly created wartime agencies such as the Office of War Information and the Office of Strategic Services. As the United States Forces spread globally, the need for the accurate and current information of the far corners of the world multiplied, and government researchers tried to obtain the best information available from the books and periodicals in the collections of the Library of Congress.

The Library of Congress has probably the world's most enviable acquisition arrangement so far as the domestic publications are concerned, because the Library automatically receives two copies of each publication published in the United States as the copyright deposit. Books the Library buys are usually books from foreign countries. Acquisitions of foreign books prior to the war usually paralleled the main lines of the scholarly orthodoxy. The war provided the Library of Congress the occasion for the most critical evaluation of the contents of its collections from the standpoint of national need. This evaluation made a tremendous impact on the postwar acquisition policies of the Library of Congress.

Limiting my observation to the Orientalia collections of the Library of Congress, the Chinese Collection was predominantly oriented to Sinological interest, because of the long tradition of Sinology in the Western nations. Some Sinologists considered history later than the Ming Dynasty not worth studying. Such a collection was disappointing to wartime researchers who were predominantly looking for accurate and current information on the physical, geographical, social, and political conditions, as well as natural resources of contemporary China. Compared to the Chinese Collection, the Japanese Collection of the Library of Congress was not fully Japanologically oriented, because Japanology in the pre-war America was only in its formative stage. Thus, although the Japanese Collection was small, it served as a working research collection. The most well-known by-product of the wartime use of the Japanese Collection of the Library of Congress was the Chrysanthemum and the Sword by Ruth Benedict who was a research scholar in the Office of War Information.

Perhaps it was from the wartime experiences of the inadequacy of the Far Eastern language collections, that the American academic world definitely shifted from the prewar emphasis on Sinology and Japanology to the postwar emphasis on the Chinese studies and the Japanese studies.

The termination of the war did not immediately restore the former acquisition channel of the Japanese publications. It took six years before the Library of Congress reestablished normal relation with Japanese publishers.

In the meantime, the Japanese Collection increased rapidly thanks to the transfers of materials made to the Library by other government agencies. Since around April 1946 and for the duration of the Occupation of Japan, the Civil Information and Education Section of the Supreme Commander for the Allied Powers, transferred to the Library postwar monographs and periodicals. Obviously Japanese publishers were required to file each copy of their publications with CI&E for the exact purpose I do not know. They came first as a trickle, later in large volume at irregular intervals. This transfer from CI&E was not so extensive as that which the University of Maryland received from the Office of Censorship. Nevertheless, it was the only source of postwar publications for the Library of Congress during the occupation period.

While the Civil Information and Education Section favored the Library with postwar publications, the Washington Document Center assisted the Library to increase its Japanese Collection enormously by transferring approximately 300,000 volumes of prewar and wartime publications. When the Occupation troops landed in Japan, military installations throughout Japan were secured, and weapons, books and documents were captured. Books and documents were assembled in Tokyo, and eventually shipped to the Washington Document Center in Washington, D.C. After those having the military interest were removed for the retention by WDC, the entire collection was roughly separated into publications and documents. Publications were transferred to the Library of Congress, and documents were sent to the National Archives in 1947 and 1948.

Inasmuch as the Library lacked sufficient staff to sort this vast collection, consisting of humanities, social sciences, science and technology, as well as propaganda literature, and government publications, from early Tokugawa to World War II periods, the libraries of the country maintaining Japanese collections were invited to send representatives to assist in sorting the vast quantity of materials with the understanding that in return for their cooperation they could receive duplicates identified during the sorting process. During the summers of 1949 and 1950, eight librarians and students from five univeristies were engaged in the task of sorting the collection, identifying and segregating duplicates as they went along. Nearly 70,000 volumes of duplicates were shipped to the cooperating libraries. Another 20,000 volumes, largely elementary science and technology books, which were declared to be surplus to the Library, were later transferred to the Department of the Army, and eventualy turned over to the University of the Ryukyus.

A microfilming project for acquisition of foreign materials was also an outstanding development of the early post-war period. The Library transferred $52,000 to the Department of the State for the microfilming project in Tokyo from November 1948 to June 1951 of the Archives of the Japanese Ministry of Foreign Affairs. Two experts were hired by the Department of State to supervise the selection of documents. Eventually, two million feet of microfilm were taken and the <u>Checklist</u> was published by the Library in 1953.

It was in 1951 that the Library finally found that the time was ripe to implement the new post-war acquisition procedure on Japanese publications. The new procedure was called the blanket order system, devised as the result of careful evaluation of the Library's foreign language collections from the standpoint of national needs. It is a device to ensure a full coverage of the current publications subject only to the limitation of the authorized fund. The blanket order system is employed by the Library in countries where the national bibliography, such as the Nōhon shūhō of Japan, is published.

When the Soviet Union successfully orbited its Sputnik I around the earth on October 4, 1957, mankind entered the space age. Stunned by the feat, the United States poured money, manpower, and energy for the next decade not only to catch up but also to surpass the Soviet space program. The by-product of this frantic effort in the United States was two-fold: information explosion and automated bibliograhical control.

Supported by ample funding, research institutes and universities acquired a great number of pertinent publications both domestic and foreign on one hand, and produced on the other a great number of research publications of their own. When the libraries of those institutions and universities sent to the Library of Congress orders for printed cards for those publications, the Library could not supply nearly half of them. That meant that the Library did not own those publications, because the Library was not a recipient of any of the emergency research fund of the Federal Government. Once realizing this situation, Congress acted swiftly, instructing the Library of Congress to acquire "all library materials currrently published throughout the world which are of value to scholarship" and to provide "catalog information for those materials promptly after receipt", and to distribute this "bibliographic information by printing catalog cards and by other means."

By enacting this legislation in 1965, Congress fully recognized the importance of granting Federal Government aid and assistance toward solving the national problem of cataloging, especially of foreign-language materials, and gave the Library of Congress a clear mandate to provide new and unparalleled services for the benefit of other libraries. The Library entered into a cooperative arrangement with a number of national libraries of the world to use their descriptive cataloging of their books as part of the Library of Congress catalog card data. Since the Library shared those foreign cataloging data, this cooperative venture was called shared cataloging. In 1966 Shared Cataloging Offices were open in London, Wiesbaden, Oslo, and Vienna. In 1968 the Tokyo Office was established with the full cooperation of the National Diet Library. Today there are 15 centers throughout the world, of which field directors are in residentce in 8 centers, including Tokyo.

In Tokyo our office is located in the Shin Nichibo Building of the Japan Publications Trading Company which is our blanket order dealer since 1968. As a matter of fact, we lease the office and services of 9 employees of the Japan Publications Trading Company. After ten years the National Program for Acquisitions and Cataloging operations in Tokyo has attained highly efficient routine. We ship to Washington approximately 280 volumes of books by air mail every week.

The Japanese Collection in the Library of Congress is now 580,000 volumes, the largest outside of Japan, highly regarded for the quality of its content. It is used by American scholars of Japanese studies as the last resort collection.   1979.

UNIVERSITY OF MARYLAND

East Asia Collection

University of Maryland, East Asia Collection
Established in 1964
College Park, Maryland 20742

I. **Background**
    Faculty: 5, plus 2 visiting researchers
    Graduate students: 3 Ph.D. candidates
    Undergraduates: —

II. **Organization**
1. Location: Fourth floor of McKelden Library
2. Holdings: February 1980
   a) <u>Monographs:</u> 27,787 cataloged volumes, plus about 25,000 uncataloged volumes, a total of about 52,787 volumes, representing 20,837 titles.
   <u>Major subject distribution in percentages:</u>
   Hist. = 25%   Lang. & Lit.= 37%   Soc. Sci. = 20%

L.C. Classification	Number of Titles
General works, Bibliography	509
Philosophy	865
Religion	686
History	4,916
Japanese History, 2,891	
Geography	360
Social Science, Economics, Sociology	2,785
Political Science	780
Law	3
Education	590
Music	60
Fine Arts	521
Language & Literature	7,637
Japanese Lang. & Lit., 6,948	
Science & Technology	680
Military Science	445
Total	20,837

Japanese Monographs Cataloged (to 1976)

Year of Publication	No. of Vols.	%
1930-39	1,276	6.5
1940-45	1,791	9.2
1946-49	11,009	56.3
1950-59	982	5.1
1960-69	3,047	15.1
1970-75	663	3.4
Total	19,568	95.6

b) <u>Microfilm:</u> 9 titles in 340 reels
c) <u>Periodical subscriptions:</u> 139
d) <u>Document files:</u> Part of the Gordon W. Prange Collection is 24

four-drawer file cabinets containing censored documents (magazines, books, newspapers). Two file cabinets contain the papers of Justin Williams, Sr.
3. Staff: 2.6 professionals, 2 paraprofessionals, 1.5 student, 2 temporary staff. The Head of the East Asia Collection, a Japan specialist, reports to the Associate Librarian for Public Service.

III. Collection Management
1. Classification system: L.C.
2. Shelving of books: separately by language
3. Public catalog: cards are interfiled in the main public catalog. Shelf list is separated by language.
4. Book selection: Japanese bibliograher, recommendations of faculty.
5. Acquisitions: Data not kept by the East Asia Collection; titles are counted only when the books are cataloged.
6. Cataloging: Original cataloging retained for pre-1958 imprints; modified L.C. cards in use since 1958.

1976-77	991 vols.
1977-78	1,194 vols.
1978-79	1,838 vols.
6/79-12/79	954 vols.

7. Circulation: Open Hours: M - Th, 8 am - 11 pm; F, 8 am - 6 pm; Sa, 10 am - 6 pm; Su, Noon - 11 pm.
    Sample Circulation Figures: July - December, 1979
        Checkout Slips (returned from the General Library to the EA Collection)

Humanities		
	History	28
	Art	5
	Religion	3
	Lang. & Lit.	135
Social Sciences		
	Economics	9
	Political Science	1
	Sociology	2
	Education	4
Science, Technology		6
Bibliography		11
Total		204

    Periodical and newspaper use (including Chinese, Japanese, and Korean): by students, 716; by faculty/staff, 652; by visitors, 273.
    Photoduplication requests: over 2,000 pages of Prange Collection materials.
    Interlibrary loans: handled by the General Library; no figures available for the East Asia Collection.
8. Financing:
    a) Allocation for Chinese, Japanese, and Korean language books and Western language reference works (an estimated 50 percent of the book budget, 70 percent

of the periodical budget, and 75 percent of the standing order budget are for Japanese language materials):

	1978-79	1979-80
Books, monographs	$10,000	$19,100
Periodical maintenance	7,850	10,975
New periodicals	400	850
Standing order maintenance	4,050	5,500
New standing orders	1,250	1,650
Total	$23,550*	$37,895

* Japan World Exposition Commemorative Fund one-time grant of $10,000 for 1978-79. An additional $4,700 was allocated by the library from a special budget to cover the difference between the actual cost of "Expo" books ($14,700) and the award ($10,000). Probable expenditures for 1979-80, <u>Japanese collection</u>, were $23,963.

b) <u>Salaries:</u> 1978-79 total, $83,308.

University of Maryland   February, 1980

"1978 and 1979 have been years of significant growth and accomplishment for the University of Maryland's East Asia Collection..." writes Frank Shulman in the February, 1980 issue of the CEAL Bulletin. One sign of this growth is the Prange Collection, which is comprised of books, periodicals, newspapers, and various broadsides, as well as censored items. They were collected by the Civil Information and Education Section of the Allied Occupation Headquarters of Japan and were brought to the United States and the University Library by Dr. Gordon W. Prange, former Chief of the History section of the General Headquarters. Almost twenty years after its arrival in this country, the Prange Collection was formally named in May, 1979. The usefulness of this special collection was augmented by a gift of the personal papers of Dr. Justin Williams, former chief of the Government Section of the SCAP Legislative Division.

The second event of note was the acquisition by the library of a spacious reading room with adjoining offices; 27,787 cataloged Japanese books, and Chinese and Korean books are shelved on the mezzanine level above the reading room.

The following articles (along with 27 others in Japanese periodicals) explain the East Asia Collection and its special features:

Hopewell, Jim. 1971. Press censorship: a case study." Argus 6:19-20, 58-64.

Kim, Hong H. 1979. Scholar's guide to Washington, D.C. for East Asian Studies (China, Japan, Korea, and Mongolia). Washington, D.C.: Smithsonian Institution Press. (Contains an entry for the University of Maryland East Asia Collection.)

Shulman, Frank Joseph. 1978. Publications and unpublished materials from the Allied Occupation of Japan within the East Asia Collection, McKeldin Library, University of Maryland, College Park. CEAL Bulletin 55:43-48. (Condensed version published in 1978 under the title "Materials from the Allied Occupation of Japan in the East Asia Collection, U.M." The Crab 7:5.

Shulman, Frank Joseph. 1980. East Asia Collection, University of Maryland Libraries (College Park). CEAL Bulletin, February. (This article with a few modifications was published in The occupation of Japan: economic policy and reform. The Proceeding of a Symposium Sponsored by the MacArthur Memorial, at the Onmi International Hotel in Norfolk, Virgina, April, 1978.)

UNIVERSITY OF MICHIGAN

Asia Library

University of Michigan, Asia Library
Established in 1948
Ann Arbor, Michigan   48109

I. Background
    Faculty: 22
    Graduate students: 736 in East Asian Studies, plus 35 teaching staff, including 100 Japanese Studies majors.
    Undergraduates: 1,413 in East Asian Studies, including 15 Japanese Studies majors.

II. Organization
  1. Location: Fourth floor of Harlan Hatcher Graduate Library
  2. Holdings: 1979
    a) <u>Monographs</u>: 148,838 volumes, including 4,000 volumes of the Kamada collection to be recataloged and 750 pre-cataloged current acquisitions. The Law Library has about 9,300 volumes. Total: 158,138+ volumes. In titles: 53,492 titles in 144,088 cataloged volumes.

Major subject distribution in percentages:
Hist. = 30%   Lang. & Lit.= 25%   Soc. Sci. = 25%

L.C. Classification	Titles
General works	1,090
Philosophy	685
Religion (Buddhism, 1,355)	2,220
History	15,275
Japanese History, 11,851	
Geography, etc.	825
Social Science, Economics, Sociology	9,487
Political Science	1,970
Law (plus 9,300 vols. in Law Library)	650
Education	1,411
Music	249
Fine Arts	1,879
Language & Literature	13,190
Japanese Language, 2,028	
Japanese Literature, 9,323	
Science & Technology	2,115
Military Science	528
Bibliography	1,918
Total	53,492

    b) <u>Microfilm</u>: 5,550 reels
    c) <u>Microfiche</u>: 5,041 sheets
    d) <u>Periodical subscriptions</u>: 944 titles, including annuals
    e) <u>Newspaper subscriptions</u>: 3 dailies by air
    f) <u>Pamphlet files</u>: 150 boxes
    g) <u>Document files</u>: 3 four-drawer cabinets

3. Staff: 3.5 professionals, 2 clericals, 1.5 student help. Staff reports to the Head of the Asia Library, who reports to the Associate Director for Public Service.

III. Collection Management
1. Classification system: L.C.
2. Shelving of books: shelved separately from main library holdings; intershelved regardless of language within Asia Library.
3. Public catalog: two main catalogs—Chinese and Japanese-Korean books—and a small catalog of Western language books are located in the Asia Library Reading Room. Both the Chinese and Japanese-Korean catalogs serve as a union catalog of books in those languages in various libraries on the University of Michigan campus.
4. Book selection: Japanese bibliographer, requests from professors and users.
5. Acquisitions:

	1974-78	1978-79	7-12, 1979
monographs	19,801v.	4,615v.	2,477v.
serials			653t.

(9 titles added, 2 suspended)

6. Cataloging: 7-12, 1979

	6-month Total	Monthly Average
No. of titles cataloged	1,248	208
added	790	131.6
by L.C. cards	1,163	194
other library cards	17	2.8
original cataloging	68	11.3
recataloged	191	31.8

7. Circulation: Open hours: M - Th, 8 am - midnight; F, 8 am - 10 pm; Sa, 10 am - 6 pm; Su, 1 pm - midnight.

In 1978-79, total East Asia Library charges, including Chinese, Japanese, and Korean materials, amounted to 8,733 items.

Sample circulation figures: Returned slips, 9-12, 1979, Japanese

by students	541 items
by faculty/staff	101 items
by visitors	95 items
interlibrary loans	78 items
Total	815 items

Subject Distribution	Items
History	127
Language & Literature	475
Art	54
Religion	19
Economics	30
Political Science	19
Sociology	27
Others	64
Total	815

There were 1,211 items charged out as of December 30, 1979, of which 77% were on humanities and 23% on social sciences.
Interlibrary loans: 7/79 - 3/80
499 loans, of which 2/3 were Japanese books, sent to 62 libraries in the United States and 6 foreign countries.
Photoduplication services: free of charge up to 50 pages.

8. Financing: 1979-80
   a) Book budget:

University Library, Japanese book budget (includes subscriptions and continuations)		$50,000
Outside funds:		$36,000
Government (NDEA)	$17,626	
Foundations	$18,374	
Gifts		$16,500
Total		$102,500

   b) Salaries: Total for 7.0 staff: $91,596
   c) Other expenses: 150 copies of bi-monthly acquisitions list, office supplies and equipment ($2,500 in 79/80), binding ($1,500), and transportation for professional conferences paid from University Library funds.
   d) Library service grants: Travel funds to assist non-Michigan scholars to come to Ann Arbor to use the library and funds for copying scholarly materials are available; 23 grantees in a year. Funds are occasionally available for travel expenses for liaison with area libraries.

University of Michigan   July 1979

The Asia Library is located on the 4th floor of the Graduate Library; its facilities include administrative offices, a reading room, stacks, and an area for processing books, where the daily tasks of handling the books, from ordering and receiving to cataloging and servicing, are carried out, mainly for the Asia Library, but also for other special libraries on the campus. Books in Chinese, Japanese and Korean are intershelved in the stacks according to the L.C. classification system, which was adopted when the Japanese collection was begun in the early 1950's. The public catalog, however, is divided by languages, and 25 volumes of printed catalogs were published in 1978, 12 for Japanese and Korean.

Although the building of the Japanese collection began only after the War, its holdings include the Bartlett* collection of about 140 pre-Meiji

---

* About the Bartlett collection: See the special number dedicated to the memory of Harley Harris Bartlett, 1886-1960, of the Asa Gray Bulletin, N.S. Vol. III. Spring, 1961, nos. 3-4. Edited and published for the Gray Memorial Botanical Association and the Botanical Gardens Association of the University of Michigan, by Rogers McVaugh. vi, 267p.

illustrated books, manuscripts and maps relating to botany, and the Kamada collection, formerly part of a local public library on Shikoku Island. The latter provided pre-war standard works on all subjects, as well as some rare books. Most of the Kamada collection has been recataloged and is shelved as part of the general Asia Library collection, leaving about 4,000 volumes to be recataloged. The library also acquired a manuscript collection of about 8,000 scripts of Japanese folk dramas gathered in various regions between 1946 and 1949 under the Occupation Government, and these should provide an interesting source for the study of ethno-linguistics. One of the most frequently used special collections is that of the M.A. theses presented to the Department of Far Eastern Languages and Literature, and to the Center for Japanese Studies. Though incomplete, the collection includes about 250 theses. The Japanese collection contains some reference books in the Western languages, but books on Japan in Western languages are located in the Undergraduate and/or Graduate Library. However, some of the important documents on World War II and the Occupation, such as records of the military tribunal, the Hussey papers, and combat reports, etc., are kept in the Asia Library.

The University of Michigan Law School Library holds about 8,000 volumes of basic documents and treatises, some 50 titles of reviews, and about 1,300 uncataloged items, mostly gifts of the late Professor George, and from other sources. When the Asia Library purchases books which are primarily of interest to the Law Library, the catalog cards for these are sent to be filed in their public catalog as well. In recent years there have been several law students with a special interest in Japan, and about 15 Japanese law students have attended the University of Michigan by special arrangement.

Publications of the Asia Library Concerning Japan

An annotated select list of Japanese labor statistical materials, postwar to the present. 1977.

Asia Library: User's Guide. 1979.

Catalogs of the Asia Library, Japanese language. Boston, G.K. Hall, 1978. 12 v.

Hussey papers: A checklist. 1977.

List of Japanese bibliographies. Bibliographical series III, 1966.

Local studies of Japan: Hokkaido, Sakhalin, and the Kurile Islands. Bibliograhical series I, 1965.

A select list of books on the history of education in Japan and A select list of periodicals on education. 1976.

A select list of books on Tokyo, 1868-1971. 1975.

A select list of Japanese serials currently received in the Asia Library. 1973.

Selective list of new acquisitions. Bimonthly.

UNIVERSITY OF MINNESOTA

East Asian Library

University of Minnesota, East Asian Library
Established in 1965
Wilson Library, Minneapolis, Minnesota 55455

I. Background
- Faculty: 9
- Graduate students: 12
- Undergraduates: not available

II. Organization
1. Location: Sub-basement of the Wilson Memorial Library, West Bank campus
2. Holdings: 1980
   a) <u>Monographs</u>: 18,290 volumes, including about 200 uncataloged volumes, representing 6,200 titles.

   Major subject distribution in percentages:
   Hist. = 22%   Lang. & Lit.= 45%   Soc. Sci. = 17%

L.C. Classification	Titles
General works, Bibliography	128
Philosophy	127
Religion	213
History	1,548
Japanese History, 542	
Geography	99
Social Science, Economics	739
Sociology, 146	
Political Science	140
Law	30
Education	145
Music	22
Fine Arts	125
Language & Literature	2,847
Japanese Language, 600	
Japanese Literature, 2,565	
Science & Technology	26
Military Science	11
Total	6,200

   b) <u>Microfilm</u>: 168 reels (included in the holdings)
   c) <u>Serials</u>: 226 titles, including current subscriptions
   d) <u>Newspapers</u>: 1 daily by sea mail
3. Staff: No Japanese staff—1 Chinese professional, .5 paraprofessional, some Japanese student help. Head of the East Asian Library, a Chinese specialist, reports to the Director of the Wilson Library.

III. Collection Management
1. Classification system: L.C.
2. Shelving of books: intershelved regardless of language; separate shelving for periodicals.
3. Public catalog: interfiled; located in East Asian Library reading room.

4. Book selection: recommendations of professors
5. Acquisitions:

	1970/75	75/76	76/77	77/78	78/79	79/80
Monographs	1,945v.	756v.	557v.	458v.	488v.	540v.
Serials						120t.
Microfilm			168 reels			

Last ten years, average increase: 760 volumes per year
Last five years, average increase: 520 volumes per year

6. Cataloging: Cataloging done in the Central Technical Service, with a 70% use of L.C. cards. Original cataloging occupies about 20% of the cataloger's time for both Chinese and Japanese books.
7. Circulation: Open hours: MWF, 9 am - 5 pm; TTh, 9 am - 7 pm; Sa, 10 am - 5 pm.
Total circulation in 1979-80 amounted to 6,254 charges, with a ratio of 3 Japanese to 7 Chinese books used.
8. Financing: 1980-81
    a) Book budget:
        University Library funds for East Asian Library
            Monographs (65-70% Japanese books) $14,000
            Periodicals $6,000
        Total $20,000
    b) Salaries: East Asian Library total: $69,000
    c) Other expenses: Binding for East Asian Library ($3,104) from University Library funds.

University of Minnesota   July, 1980

Established in 1965, the East Asia Collection is housed in the sub-basement of the Wilson Memorial Library for the humanities and social sciences on the West Bank Campus, and occupies a corner room adjoining two other libraries—the South Asia Library, which houses the nationally known English language collection on India, and the Middle East library. The East Asia Collection contains books and periodicals in Chinese, Japanese, Korean, and other languages of the Far East, as well as a small number of reference works in English on those countries.

A professional librarian, reporting to the Director of the Wilson Library, administers the operation and activities of the East Asia Collection with the help of one full-time library assistant and part-time student assistants. Plans have been made to add a professional full-time cataloger in Central Technical Services for the 1980-81 academic year.

Of the 76,000 volumes in the collection, 18,290 or 23 percent are in Japanese. The users include nine faculty members, about twelve graduate students concentrating on subjects having to do with Japan, and many undergraduate students who are not required to use Japanese language books but who sometimes ask the librarian to translate passages for them. For its over-all size, this collection boasts an outstanding section of poetry (479 titles), especially books on the Manyōshū (255 titles).

OHIO STATE UNIVERSITY

East Asian Collection

Ohio State University, East Asian Collection
Established in 1962
1858 Neil Avenue, Columbus, Ohio 43210

I. Background
    Faculty: 8
    Graduate students: 24 (1978-79) East Asia
    Undergraduates: 668 East Asia

II. Organization
  1. Location: Second floor, Main Library
  2. Holdings: June, 1980
    a) <u>Monographs</u>: 12,476 cataloged volumes and an unknown number of uncataloged materials; holdings in 1979 totaled 3,342 titles in 10,971 volumes.

Major subject distribution in percentages:
Hist. = 21%   Lang. & Lit. = 56%   Soc. Sci. = 12%

L.C. Classification	Titles
General works, Bibliography	91
Philosophy	20
Religion	85
History	641
Japanese History, 550	
Geography	64
Social Science, Economics, Sociology	320
Political Science	44
Law	4
Education	37
Music	7
Fine Arts	73
Language & Literature	1,870
Japanese Language, 265	
Japanese Literature, 1,489	
Science & Technology	72
Military Science	14
Total	3,342

    b) <u>Microfilm</u>: 563 reels
    c) <u>Periodical subscriptions</u>: 62 titles
    d) <u>Newspaper subscriptions</u>: 1 title
  3. Staff: Two professionals (one the Head of the East Asian Library, and one cataloger) each devote half time to Japanese language materials. One clerical (Japanese) for computer searching. The Head of the EAL reports to the Assistant Head for Collection Building.

III. Collection Management
  1. Classification system: L.C.
  2. Shelving of books: intershelved with general library holdings
  3. Public catalog: cataloged by OCLC in romanized entries. Characters for author and title are given for one set of computer print-out

cards, and used as main entry cards in the public catalog.
4. Book selection: blanket order to Japan Publications Trading Co. (JPTC), and recommendations of professors.
5. Acquisitions:
   1978-79   monographs: 650v. (estimate)
              serials, subscriptions: 62 items
   1979-80   monographs: 1,029v.
6. Cataloging: 8/79 - 2/79
   Estimated total: 2,500 volumes cataloged
   By L.C. cards: 90%
   By original cataloging: 100 titles per month, 6 serials

   Remarks: Precataloged books and periodical sets, as of February 19, 1979, totaled about 2,000 titles in 2,500-2,550 volumes. Cataloging by OCLC in romanized entries: one set in the general catalog has characters written for main author and title entries. About 30 titles/day cataloged through the OCLC type of NUC.
7. Circulation: Open hours: open when University Library is open; reference service hours are M - F, 8 am - 4 pm.
   The circulation system is computerized; separate figures for the EAL are not available. About 26 faculty members and 700 students are regular users.
8. Financing: 1978-79
   a) <u>Book budget</u>:
   University Book Fund: East Asia Fund for
      blanket order to JPTC $8,235
   University Library serials fund   1,907
      Total (Japanese publications) $10,142

   Estimated price of monographs: $20-23/vol.
   Estimated price of serial subscription: $27-31/title

   b) <u>Salaries</u>: 1979-80 (for Japan) Total: $26,836

Ohio State University   February, 1979
Oriental Studies East Asian Collection

There is no Japanese bibliographer for this collection. Books are selected according to instruction which accompany an annual blanket order to the Japan Publications Trading Company. Books are intershelved in the University's general library collection, and cataloging is done by the main department. Within this department, the original cataloging of Japanese books is done by a professional librarian responsible for the East Asia collection in this area, with about half of her time being spent on Japanese books.

Within the University's computerized catalog-the "Que" section of the general catalog department—books are classified by OCLC and NUC by romanized titles and author names, etc. One set of the computer print-out cards have characters added to them, and these are filed in the East Asia public catalog.

Publications

The development of the East Asian collection in the OSU Library.

List of East Asian Reference books held in the OSU Library, November 15, 1978. Part 1: List of reference books held in the EAL reading room. Part 2: List of reference books held in the reference department.

List of periodicals in the fields of Chinese and Japanese studies held in the OSU Library. Part 1: Chinese. Part 2: Japanese. Part 3: selected titles in Western languages. June 1, 1974.

Selective list of Chinese and Japanese accessions to the OSU Library. Lists precatalog books: part 1, Chinese; part 2, Japanese. Nos. 13-14, June and December 1978.

Collection: Within the total of 10,971 volumes at the time of the survey, some 2000-2500 items remained uncataloged, as against 3362 cataloged titles. The percentage of uncataloged items is large enough within this comparatively small collection that it is difficult to assess the adequacy of the holdings within several of the subject classes. However, the section on language and literature, especially modern literature, is strong, and could be maintained as a special feature of this collection.

UNIVERSITY OF OREGON

Japanese Collection

University of Oregon, Japanese Collection
Established in 1967
Eugene, Oregon 97403

I. Background
Faculty: 6 (plus 7 EA area faculty)
Enrollment: figures not available

II. Organization
1. Location: General Library Reference Room
2. Holdings: March, 1979
    a) Monographs: 15,634 volumes, including 234 uncataloged current volumes, representing 5,352 cataloged titles.

    Major subject distribution in percentages:
    Hist. = 23%   Lang. & Lit.= 30%   Soc. Sci. = 11%

L.C. Classification	Titles
General works	90
Philosophy	125
Religion (Buddhism, 107)	612
History	1,581
Japanese History, 1,219	
Geography	100
Social Science, Economics, Sociology	361
Political Science	130
Law	50
Education	65
Music	13
Fine Arts	350
Language & Literature	1,584
Japanese Language, 205	
Japanese Literature, 1,185	
Science & Technology	91
Military Science	42
Bibliography	150
Total	5,352

    b) Microfilm: 5 titles on 96 reels
    c) Periodicals: 118 titles
    d) Newspapers: 1 title
    e) Pamphlet files: none, except that biographical and bibliographical information accompanying sets of monographs are bound at the Catalog Department and treated as new titles.

3. Staff: .6 professional, .05 student help. Staff reports to the Director of the Libraries, as all professional staff members are directly under the Director. In 1980-81, the part-time professional's duties will become a full-time Japanese bibliographer's position.

III. **Collection Management**
  1. Classification system: L.C.
  2. Shelving of books: On open shelves in the General Library Reference Room, separated by language.
  3. Public catalog: cards interfiled with Western language cards
  4. Book selection: Japanese librarian, recommendations of faculty
  5. Acquisitions:
Monographs	1973-77	3,984 vols.
	1977-78	945 vols.
	7/78-2/79	334 vols.
Continuations		19 titles
Serials, subscriptions		118 items
  6. Cataloging: 1977-78
Monographs	345 titles
Added volumes	649 vols.
By L.C. cards	198
Original cataloging	147
Recataloged	49
  7. Circulation: Open hours: M - Th, 8 am - 11 pm; F, 8 am - 6 pm; Sa, 9 am - 5 pm; Su, Noon - 11 pm.
     Circulation is handled by general circulation; no separate figures available.
  8. Financing: 1978-79
     a) <u>Book budget</u>:
University Library, monographs	$6,350
$3,750 from Asian Studies allocation	
$1,500 from East Asian Lang. Dept. allocation	
$1,100 from History Dept. allocation	
University Library, subscriptions, serials, and continuations	$5,320
Outside funds	$1,500
Total	$13,170
     b) <u>Salaries</u>: Total (.85 FTE), $11,660
     c) <u>Other expenses</u>: Travel allowance of $400 per year if bibliographer is giving a paper or invited to participate in a panel.

University of Oregon   March, 1979

The Collection, displayed on open shelves, is located in the General Library Reference Room. Current periodicals are kept on shelves in the reading area of this room.

Catalog cards are interfiled in the public catalog with Western language books, in separate sections according to author, title, and subject. The title catalog is used as the official catalog for filing order slips with "in process" records. The subject catalog has been closed since the summer of 1975, and has been kept since that time on COM Fiche Catalog. Patrons using the subject catalog must refer to at least three sections to make a complete search of a given subject: the Frozen Card Catalog (pre-1975); COM Fiche Cumulated Catalog (1975 to the beginning of current academic year) and COM Fiche Current Catalog (current academic year only). The author catalog will be closed in the near future. The closed catalogs are transferred to fiches and distributed to each reference desk in the main library, as well as branch libraries, together with the COM Fiche Current catalogs for public use.

Administration:

All the professional librarians, including the Japanese librarian, are immediately responsible to the Director of the Libraries, although they are encouraged to communicate closely with their respective department heads. Because of the limited size of the Japanese Collection, the Japanese librarian is required to divide her time between it and the general library, in proportions of 60 percent and 40 percent respectively. Responsibilities for the Japanese Colleciton include the teaching of a course in Japanese bibliography for one term each year.

The clerical work of ordering, receiving, and accessioning monographs and continuations, and checking periodicals to send to the bindery, is done by the General Library staff.

UNIVERSITY OF PENNSYLVANIA

East Asian Collection

University of Pennsylvania, East Asian Collection
Established in 1938
34th and Walnut Streets, Philadelphia, Pennsylvania 19174

I. Background
Faculty: 5
Graduate students: 27 East Asia
Undergraduates: 114 East Asia

II. Organization
1. Location: Fifth floor of the Van Pelt Library
2. Holdings:
    a) <u>Monographs</u>: 25,000 volumes, including 1,300 volumes to be recataloged and 300 uncataloged books, representing 7,219 cataloged titles.

    Major subject distribution in percentages:
    Hist. = 26%   Lang. & Lit.= 30%   Soc. Sci. = 12%

L.C. Classification (changing from H-Y)	Titles
General works, Bibliography	333
Philosophy, Religion	790
History	1,685
Geography	166
Social Science, Economics, Sociology	588
Political Science	198
Education	77
Music	34
Fine Arts	146
Language & Literature	2,988
Japanese Literature, 2,257	
Science & Technology	176
Military Science	38
Total	7,219

    b) <u>Microfilm</u>: 789 reels
    c) <u>Periodicals</u>: 74 subscriptions
    d) <u>Newspapers</u>: 2 titles

3. Staff: 2 Japanese clericals, under the catalog department.

III. Collection Management
1. Classification system: L.C. (Reclassification from H-Y system in progress)
2. Shelving of books: separated by language within the East Asian Collection.
3. Public catalog: cards interfiled with main library holdings
4. Book selection: no new titles, budget is to cover continuations, periodical subscriptions.

5. Acquisitions:
    Monographs   1974-78   1,500 vols.
                   1978-79   90 vols.
                   7-12/79   120 vols.
    Serials   1979   74 titles
6. Cataloging: (No new monographs acquired)
    Added volumes (by L.C. cards):
        1978-79   323
        7-12, 1979   276
    Recataloged (original cards)
        1978-79   329
        7-12, 1979   276
7. Circulation: Open hours: M - Th, 8:45 am - Midnight; F, 8:45 am - 10 pm; Sa, 10 am - 6 pm; Su, Noon - Midnight. Circulation figures not available.
8. Financing: 1979-80
    a) <u>Book budget:</u>
        Japanese book budget (estimate) $10,000
        Subscriptions   3,000
        Total $13,000
    b) <u>Salaries:</u> 2 Staff, total: $20,000

University of Pennsylvania   January, 1980

    The Japanese collection of about 25,000 volumes is a part of the East Asia Collection, located on the 5th floor of the Van Pelt Library, the university's main library. The East Asia seminar room, which adjoins the stacks, is used as a reading room and has Chinese, Japanese and Korean language reference books, journals and the author-title card catalog for the three languages. Although books are shelved separately from the main collection, the shelf list is interfiled with the main shelf list so that the East Asia library books will be included in the library's automated system. Consequently, the Japanese catalogers have desks in the Catalog Department and work under the supervision of its head. In recent years, no new Japanese titles have been ordered except those which are continuations of series. This arrangement is necessarily temporary until some definite plan for the future of the collection is decided.

UNIVERSITY OF PITTSBURGH

East Asian Library

University of Pittsburgh, East Asian Library
Established in 1960
Pittsburgh, Pennsylvania 15260

I. Background
Faculty: 6
Enrollment: figures not available

II. Organization
1. Location: Second floor of Hillman Library
2. Holdings:
    a) <u>Monographs:</u> 12,138 volumes (plus 750-1,000 uncataloged volumes and unbound periodicals) representing 4,301 titles.

    Major subject distribution in percentages:
    Hist. = 43%   Lang. & Lit.= 20%   Soc. Sci. = 23%

L.C. Classification	Titles
General works, Bibliography	145
Philosophy, Religion	315
History	1,657
Japanese History, 1,401	
Geography	174
Social Science, Economics, Sociology	845
Political Science	34
Law	55
Education	60
Music	8
Fine Arts	70
Language & Literature	844
Japanese Language and Literature, 781	
Science & Technology	62
Military Science	32
Total	4,301

    b) <u>Microfilm:</u> 5 titles on 506 reels
    c) <u>Periodical subscriptions:</u> 271 titles
    d) <u>Newspaper subscriptions:</u> 6 titles

3. Staff: 1 professional, .3 serial librarian, .25 catalog supervisor, .5 student. Staff reports to Head of the East Asian Library, who reports to the Director of University Libraries.

III. Collection Management
1. Classification system: L.C.
2. Shelving of books: separately by language
3. Public catalog: cards filed separtely by language
4. Book selection: requests from professors; reference books by library staff

5. Acquisitions:

Monographs	1973-77 (5 years)	4,781 vols.
	1977-78	930 vols.
Bound periodicals	1973-77	821 vols.
	1977-78	275 vols.

6. Cataloging: 1977-78
   - Monographs — 547 titles
   - Added volumes — 901 volumes
   - By L.C. cards — 473 titles
   - Original cataloging — 74 titles

   Serials are shelved in alphabetical order by titles, not classified, but cataloged, and listed in the University of Pittsburgh Library Periodicals and Serials.

7. Circulation: Open hours: M - Th, 7:50 am - 1 am; F, 7:50 am - 11:30 pm; Sa, 8:30 am - 5 pm; Su, Noon - 1 am.

   Total EAL circulation: 20,271 items. There is no way to count the number of Japanese books in this total, which includes Chinese, Japanese, Korean, and Western language books.

   Interlibrary loans: 13 monographs, 9 periodicals, 15 microfilm reels.

8. Financing:

   a) Book budget: 1977-78
   University library budget for EAL was $42,400, 53% for Chinese, 41% for Japanese, 6% for Western languages. The actual amount spent ($47,606.78) included $31,398.31 for monographs, $8,808.47 for subscriptions, and $7,400 for binding.

   Japanese expenditures:

Monographs (449 titles in 920 volumes)	$11,902
Subscriptions (88 titles)	4,433
Total	$16,337

   Average price per volume: $13.00
   Average price per periodical title: $50.38

   b) Salaries: Total (1979-80): $22,060
   c) Other expenses: binding, 275 volumes @ $11, total $3,025.

University of Pittsburgh   February, 1979

The East Asian Library is located on the second floor of the Hillman Library, in a section occupied by offices and stacks. There would seem to be little room for the Asian Library to expand beyond its present quarters, but its location offers easy access for students and in this sense may be considered strategic. The collection presents a good representative sample of books for undergraduate users, containing as it does books on East Asia in Western languages as well as in Chinese, Japanese, and Korean. The books are cataloged and classified by the Library of Congress Classification System and shelved separately by language. The public catalog is also filed separately by language.

A professional serial librarian checks in all periodicals regardless of the language; cataloging, preparing for binding, and shelving are also his responsibilties.

While Western language materials are generally outside the scope of this survey, it may be mentioned that subject areas which were not fully covered by Japanese language works were well supplemented by Western language works, which tended to complete the coverage: for example, there were a number of English books in the fine arts section. It is noted also that the fund for English materials in 1977-78 was $7,000.

Staff time: A staff member may take time away during library office hours to study at the university, but the hours must be made up, usually the same week.

PRINCETON UNIVERSITY

East Asian Collection

125

Princeton University, East Asian Collection
Established in 1926
317 Palmer Hall, Princeton, New Jersey 08540

I. Background
Faculty: 11, Japanese Studies
Graduate students: 13 Japanese studies majors
Undergraduates: 17 Japanese studies majors

II. Organization
1. Location: Second floor of Palmer-Jones Hall
2. Holdings: January, 1980
   a) <u>Monographs</u>: 70,774 volumes, including 410 uncataloged current acquisitions, representing 29,771 cataloged titles.

   Major subject distribution in percentages:
   Hist. = 28%   Lang. & Lit.= 27%   Soc. Sci. = 24%

H-Y Classification adapted to L.C.	Titles
General works, Bibliography	1,622
Philosophy	835
Religion (Buddhism, 1,374)	2,181
History	8,437
Japanese History, 3,887	
Social Science, Economics, Sociology	4,370
Political Science	1,253
Law	533
Education	925
Music, Fine Arts	797
Language & Literature	7,926
Japanese Language and Literature, 6,406	
Science, Technology, Military Science	892
Total	29,771

   b) <u>Microfilm</u>: 2,443 reels
   c) <u>Periodicals</u>: 919 titles, including 777 current subscriptions
   d) <u>Newspaper</u>: 1, by airmail
3. Staff: 3.3 professionals, 2.63 paraprofessionals, 1550 hours/year student help. Staff reports to Head, Gest Oriental and East Asian Library, who reports to the Director of the University Libraries.

III. Collection Management
1. Classification system: H-Y
2. Shelving of books: separately by language
3. Public catalog: cards filed separately by language
4. Book selection: requests from professors, Japanese catalogers
5. Acquisitions:

Monographs	1974–78	17,176	volumes
	1978–79	3,112	volumes
	6-12/79	1,438	volumes
Serials (paid)		185	titles

6. Cataloging: 1978-79
    Monographs   1,994 titles
    Added volumes   3,719 volumes
    By L.C. cards   1,285 titles
    Original cataloging   695 titles
    Recataloged   14 titles
7. Circulation: Open hours: M - F, 9 am - 11 pm; Sa, 9 am - 5 pm; Su, 2 pm - 11 pm.
    Sample circulation figures: (Sept., 1979 - Jan. 21, 1980; about 5 months' sampling) 2,299 items EA
    Interlibrary loans: 77 items
    Borrowed: 8 monographs and 10 items by photoduplication
    Lent: 56 monographs and 10 items by photoduplication
8. Financing:
    a) Book budget: 1978-79
        University Library funds $34,750
        Outside funds   14,910
        Government (NDEA)   7,500
        Japan-U.S. Friendship Commission 18,800
            Total $75,960

        Average price of serial subscription $38.54 per title
        Average price of continuations $28.89 per vol.
        Average price of monographs $26.23 per vol.

    b) Salaries: Total (1979-80) $82,805

Princeton University   January 19, 1980

The Princeton University East Asian Collection is dominated by the famous Gest Oriental Library, a collection consisting of many rare Chinese books. This fact is reflected in the combined title of Gest Oriental Library and East Asian Collections. The library is located in Palmer-Jones Hall, the second floor of Palmer Hall having been renovated to house the public catalog room, reference room, and the library offices. The third floor houses the stacks and the Gest rare book collection. One must go through the public catalog room to reach the stairs to the Chinese and Japanese stacks and the connecting hallway to the Jones Hall Library, where the periodical display, storage stacks, Western language materials, and Korean collection are located. Half of the area in Jones Hall is used by the Near East collections.

In 1960, the Japanese collection totaled some 11,000 volumes. Twenty years later, in 1980, it numbers over 70,000 volumes, growing steadily at an average of 3,000 volumes per year.

The books are shelved separately by language; therefore, the shelflist and the public catalog of the author-title and catchwords subject cards, are likewise filed separately by language.

Once inside historic Palmer-Jones Hall, one can see that the renovation of the library has been very successful, and it is a pleasant surprise to find good working space as well as a special room for the Gest rare book collection.

UNIVERSITY OF ROCHESTER

Asia Library

University of Rochester, Asia Library
Established in 1965
Rochester, New York 14627

I. **Background**
- Faculty: 5
- Graduate students: —
- Undergraduates: 390 (Asian studies)

II. **Organization**
1. Location: Fifth floor of the University Library
2. Holdings: 1979
    a) Monographs: 10,894 volumes, representing 4,873 titles

    Major subject distribution in percentages:
    Hist. = 28%   Lang. & Lit.= 30%   Soc. Sci. = 12%

L.C. Classification	Titles
General works, Bibliography	201
Philosophy, Religion	371
History, Geography	1,371
Japanese History and Geography, 1,030	
Social Sciences	600
Fine Arts	64
Language & Literature	1,844
Japanese Language and Literature, 1,638	
Science & Technology	422
Total	4,873

    b) Microfilm: a set of Asahi Shimbun
    c) Periodicals: 57 titles
3. Staff: For Asia Library, 1 professional, 2 paraprofessionals, 1 student. Head of the Asia Library reports to Assistant Director of the Reader Service.

III. **Collection Management**
1. Classification system: L.C.
2. Shelving of books: separately by language
3. Public catalog: cards filed separately by language
4. Book selection: requests of professors
5. Acquisitions: (July 1978 - May 1979; eleven months)

Monographs	202	volumes
Continuations	56	titles
Serials, subscriptions and gifts	57	items

6. Cataloging: 1978-79

Number of titles	56	
Added volumes	202	volumes
By L.C. cards	56	

7. Circulation: 1978-79
    Total circulation: 10,400 volumes for the Asia Library. Users include Japanese students and faculty members of the University of Rochester and the University of Buffalo.

8. Financing:
   a) <u>Book budget</u>:
   University Library, Asia Library allocations

Monographs	$3,340
Serial subscriptions	3,500
(about $2,500 Japanese)	
Other sources	700
Total	$7,550

University of Rochester   June, 1979

The Asia Library covers China, Japan and India, and is staffed by its head, and one full-time assistant, with part-time support by a member of the general catalog section staff. It is located on the fifth floor of the University Library, adjoining the Center for Asian Studies and has a spacious reading room containing about 3,000 volumes of reference books and a balcony for periodical displays.

Materials in the Asia Library are grouped by language within the shelf list of the catalog department. The only public catalog of the materials is the separate one in the Asia Library itself, where the cards are likewise grouped by language.

The Japanese collection has been developed to meet the needs of professors in their research and training. (The language is not required of students taking area studies courses.) The collection is good for some subjects, but for others there is no coverage at all. The allocation for book funds for the Asia Library, $3,340 in 1978-79, is so small that the head of the library must find additional funds from various other departments simply to meet the minimum needs of professors. For all its shortcomings, the Asia Library exists as a resource center where professors may have their research materials pooled for mutual use, and as such, it has an important place in the area studies program.

The University is a member of the Five Universities Consortium of Western New York State, and the library is used especially by professors from the SUNY Brockport and the University of Buffalo. It is also used quite heavily by the local Asian community.

UNIVERSITY OF TEXAS
at Austin

Asia Collection

University of Texas at Austin, Asian Collection
Established in 1960
Austin, Texas 78712

I. Background
Faculty: 7
Enrollment: figures not available

II. Organization
1. Location: Third floor of the Main Building (Tower)
2. Holdings:
    a) <u>Monographs</u>: 28,994 volumes, including about 2,000 uncataloged volumes, representing 7,085 titles.

    Major subject distribution in percentages:
    Hist. = 29%   Lang. & Lit.= 35%   Soc. Sci. = 23%

L.C. and D.C. Classification	Titles
General works, Bibliography	230
Philosophy, Religion	397
History, Geography	2,053
Japanese History, 1,524 (L.C. only)	
Social Science, Law, Education	1,600
Music, Fine Arts	64
Language & Literature	2,452
Japanese Lang. and Lit., 1,797 (L.C. only)	
Science & Technology	237
Military Science	52
Total	7,085

    Shelf list count is not complete, because of 1) the interfiling of all East Asia language cards, 2) two different classification files, and 3) a large proportion of uncataloged materials for the number of cataloged volumes. However, the percentages of books under broad subject will be close to the above figures.

    b) <u>Microfilm</u>: 2 titles on 244 reels
    c) <u>Periodical subscriptions</u>: 146
    d) <u>Newspaper subscriptions</u>: 2 (gift of Japanese Consulate in Houston)
3. Staff: .5 professional (Head of the Asian Collection), 1 paraprofessional, student help 10 hours/week. Head reports to the Director of University Libraries.

III. Collection Management
1. Classification system: D.C., 18%; L.C. 82%
2. Shelving of books: languages are intershelved
3. Public catalog: cards are interfiled
4. Book selection: professional librarian, recommendations of faculty

5. Acquisitions:

Monographs	1973-77	7,300 vols.
	1977-78	956 vols.
Continuations	1978	73 vols.
Serials and Subscriptions		146 items

6. Cataloging: 1977-78

Monographs	1,237 titles
By L.C. cards	434 titles
Original cataloging	273 titles
Recataloging	530 titles

7. Circulation: Open hours: M - F, 8 am - 5 pm. Circulation figures not available.

8. Financing: 1978-79

   a) <u>Book budget</u>:

University Library	
Japanese book fund	$10,000
Subscriptions & serials (est.)	2,482
Continuations (est.)	1,825
Total	$14,307

   Gift from Japanese consulate: 1 newspaper

   b) <u>Salaries</u>: Total (1.5 staff and student help), $20,250

University of Texas   January, 1979, Rev. Feb., 1980

The collection is part of the Oriental Library, which shares one floor with the Middle East collection. The reading room is well lighted and pleasant, the stacks are open to the public, and stack space is adequate for the collection at present. Japanese books are intershelved and cards are interfiled in the shelf list. A combined reference and information desk, and a circulation desk are each attended by one staff member, who handles business for both the Asian and Middle East collections.

The library is in the midst of changing from the Dewey Decimal classification to the Library of Congress classification. At the time of the survey, about 82 percent of the books had been reclassified.

The Head of the Asian Library oversees the book selections, original cataloging, reference services and serves as a liaison between faculty and various library services, while the paraprofessionals are responsible for technical processing, including cataloging by L.C. cards. Course work of up to three hours a week is allowed to staff members, who are not required to make up the time away from work.

Open hours are limited to nine hours per day, Monday through Friday. The library is closed on weekends, due to the fact that it is located in a separate building from the main library, and must observe the business hours of the administrative offices in the Tower whose space it shares.

The University of Texas is affiliated with the Southwest Regional Council, but 1,000 miles separates it from the nearest libraries with sizable Japanese collections such as Washington University at St. Louis or the University of Arizona at Tucson. Access to books which are not found in the University's own library must be sought at a library located at a convenient distance by air transportation.

Bibliography

Lin, Kevin. 1978. The Asian Collection. The University of Texas at Austin.

Publication

Acquisition list (irregular: for campus circulation).

UNIVERSITY OF WASHINGTON
at Seattle

East Asia Library

University of Washington at Seattle, East Asia Library
Established in 1947
Seattle, Washington 98195

I. Background
Faculty: 19
Graduate students: 24 (Japanese Studies majors)
Undergraduates: 1,409 EA

II. Organization
1. Location: Gowen Hall, the former Law School Building
2. Holdings: February 1979
   a) <u>Monographs:</u>   59,700 volumes, including 4,000 uncataloged volumes, representing 20,400 cataloged titles.

   Major subject distribution in percentages:
   Hist. = 27%   Lang. & Lit.= 28%   Soc. Sci. = 21%

H-Y Classification, adapted to L.C.	Titles
General works, Bibliography	1,268
Philosophy	507
Religion	1,039
History, Geography	5,436
Japanese History and Geography, 3,329	
Social Science, Economics, Sociology	3,048
Political Science	1,058
Law (28,000 vols. in Law Library)	
Education	258
Music, Fine Arts	1,448
Language & Literature	5,673
Japanese Language and Literature, 5,397	
Science & Technology	665
Total	20,400

   b) <u>Microfilm:</u> 139 titles on 3,945 reels
   c) <u>Periodicals:</u> 1,437 titles including 550 current titles
   d) <u>Newspapers:</u>   54 titles including 17 current titles and 1 by airmail
   e) <u>Pamphlet files:</u> 441 titles in 517 volumes
3. Staff: 1.6 professionals, 2.5 paraprofessionals, 1 student assistant. Staff reports to the Head of the East Asia Library, who reports to the Director of the University Libraries.

III. Collection Management
1. Classification system: 37% H-Y, 63% L.C.
2. Shelving of books: separately by language in H-Y classification, intershelved in L.C. classification
3. Public catalog: Japanese, Chinese, and Korean cards are interfiled; some items that are still in the H-Y classification are filed separately by language.

4. Book selection: Japanese Librarian, Assistant Head of EAL, and recommendations from professors and other users.

5. Acquisitions:
Monographs	1973-77	11,977 vols.
	1977-78	2,689 vols.
	7/78-2/79	1,520 vols.
Microfilm	1973-77	1,254 reels
	1977-78	117 reels
	7/78-2/79	19 reels

   Serial subscriptions (new periodical titles are added and paid for by the EAL for the first year, but funded thereafter by the general library):
1973-77	56 titles added
1977-78	41 titles added
2/79	550 titles

6. Cataloging: 1977-78
Number of titles	1,974
By L.C. cards	1,674
Original cataloging	300
Recataloging	128

7. Circulation: Open hours: M - Sa, 58 hours/week
   Sample circulation figures: 9-12/78 (four months' sample)
   Number of charges: 2,580 Japanese titles, 40% of EA total
   Interlibrary loans: lent, 3 items/month; borrowed, 3 items/month
   Photoduplication requests: 4 items/month
   Subject distribution of outside use (L.C. cataloged material checked out as of March 6, 1979, was used as a sample):

	Titles	Volumes
Humanities		
History	218	231
Language & Literature	477	538
Art	49	63
Religion	50	58
Other	27	33
Social Sciences		
Economics	70	98
Political Science	22	30
Sociology	61	72
Other	29	34

8. Financing:
   a) Book budget:
University Library	
Japanese book fund	$8,508
Subscriptions, serials, and continuations	20,000

	Outside funds		
	Government	7,833	
	Foundations	17,875	
	Gifts in money and books	412	
	Total	$54,628	

Remarks:	EAL	Japanese	
Library U-W	$22,690	$8,508	(3/8)
NDEA	17,000	6,375	(3/8)
NDEA	3,400	1,458	(3/7)
Mellon	5,000	1,875	(3/8)
JUSFC	15,000	15,000	
Japan Fund	1,000	1,000	
Serials	35,000	20,000	
Gift (cash)	112	112	
Gift (books)	300	300	
Total		$54,628	

Average price of monographs: $25 per volume (including mailing)
Serials subscriptions: $40 - $50 per title

b) <u>Salaries:</u> Total for 5.1 staff, $62,430
c) <u>Other expenses:</u> Book News for campus circulation, paid by the University Library; binding costs (1978-79: 1,500 volumes @ $8.00) paid by University Library; transportation to professional conferences, paid by various sources.

University of Washington, Seattle   March, 1979, Rev. June, 1980

    The East Asia Library is located in Gowen Hall, the former Law Library of the University, across from Suzallo General Library. Its spacious reading room accomodates a section of reference books and a display area for most of the current periodicals. The stacks occupy four levels in the library, which can be reached by stairs or by an elevator. An open stack system is used, except for bound serials, which are kept in the West Stack. Permission to use this area is given by the circulation desk, and a key must be checked out for temporary access. Anyone who needs assistance while working in this area may use a telephone which will connect him directly to the reference desk in the Reading Room.

    The Asia Library is one of the larger branches of the University's library system. Its head is immediately responsible to the Director of the University Libraries. The Japanese Librarian oversees one of the three area collections, the other two being Chinese and Korean. Other professional librarians supervise the serial and reference sections.

    Funding of certain aspects of the East Asia Library's operations falls outside its own allocated budget. Serials and continuations are purchased from the General Library budget. The same is true for binding costs, which are allocated by the number of volumes in the EAL; general funds pay for the binding of 2,500 volumes per year. Some bilingual publications, e.g., the census and many other statistical reports, are acquired by the General Library for its document collection.

A separate collection of about 30,000 Japanese language books on law is housed in the University Law Library. It serves as an ongoing project for the compilation of a legal history of Japan, for which additional volumes are regularly acquired, along with bulletins on current laws and regulations.

The general catalog is interfiled with cards in Japanese, Chinese and Korean, but there is a separate Japanese L.C. depository card catalog. The shelf list is interfiled according to the L.C. classification, while a number of books still listed under the Harvard-Yenching system are filed separately by language. Current acquisitions are classified by the L.C. system; until 1967 the Harvard-Yenching Table was used. Reference books, and older volumes in regular use have been reclassified, but 6,041 Japanese titles, some 32 percent of the collection, remain under the previous system. At present there are not enough staff members to reclassify the remaining volumes into the L.C. system.

University of Washington Law Library   June, 1980

Of the three collections of Japanese law books in the United States (the other two are at Harvard and at the University of Michigan), the one at the University of Washington is the largest. It is located on the fourth floor of the Law Library , and its current active users include four faculty members, nineteen law students, eight Japanese lawyers, and two American lawyers; it is open to outside users as well. There are no detailed statistics on holdings, or figures on annual acquisitions; however, in round figures the holdings number 30,000 volumes, with biennial additions of perhaps 500 new monographs, and current issues of about 600 serial subscriptions.

A Japanese librarian is responsible for the technical processing of books and serials acquired through a biennial budget, which for the years 1979-81 provided $7,300 for new monographs and $19,000 for periodical subscriptions. While the budget provides for both Chinese and Japanese materials, the emphasis of the law school courses, and hence the acquisitions program, is on Japanese materials. Books and periodicals are arranged on shelves according to a special system developed by the Japanese librarian to supplement the Japanese law section of the Library of Congress KQP classification, which has not yet been published. Circulation of materials is handled by the Law Library.

Bibliography

Chin, Teruko. 1980. Asia Library. Mimeographed. Seattle: University of Washington

Miscellaneous Bibliographies compiled by the U.W. Library's Staff on Japanese subjects (chronological order) - May 1980

1. <u>Japanese serials: holdings held at the Far Eastern Library, University of Washington Libraries.</u> By Sun S. Shin. June 17, 1970.

2. <u>Japanese government documents: a selected list.</u> By Tsuyoshi Nakamori. Sept. 15, 1970.

3. <u>A short survey of University holdings on Japanese art along with a selected bibliography of books and serials in the English language on the same subject.</u> By Marietta Ward. Feb. 1972.

4. <u>The Japanese tea esthetic; a bibliographical index.</u> By Tom Kaasa. April 1972.

5. <u>The civilizations of China, Japan, and Korea, a selective bibliography.</u> By Carla Rickerson and Tony Ferguson. Oct. 1972.

6. <u>The United States and United Nations documents on Asia.</u> By Miriam Allen and Katherine Curran. Oct. 1972.

7 <u>East Asia by Washington authors.</u> By Elise Chin. Oct. 1972.

8. <u>Selective annotated bibliography on English translations of contemporary Japanese fiction.</u> By Teruko K. Chin. Oct. 1972.

9. <u>Japanese literature; a guide to some reference sources in English.</u> By Curtis W. Stucki. Oct. 1972.

10. <u>Japanese prints; a bibliography of books, catalogs and periodical articles in the English language.</u> By Marietta Ward. Oct. 1972.

11. <u>Selective bibliography of English-language bibliographies and suggested reference works on Japanese studies, with an appended consideration of some special problems encountered in acquiring materials from Japan.</u> By Tom Kaasa. Oct. 1972.

12. Japanese studies on modern Chinese fiction. By Wen-kai Kung. Dec. 1972.

13. Zen Buddhism; a bibliography of books and articles in English, 1892-1973. By Patricia Vessie. April 1973.

14. Chin p'ing mei (an exhibit). By Teruko K. Chin and Mark W. Tam. Sept. 1973.

15. American paperback in-prints on East Asia (an exhibit). By Teruko K. Chin and Karl Lo. Nov. 1973.

16. Heike monogatari. By Teruko K. Chin. May 1978.

17. Japanese serials on business and economics currently received at East Asia Library. By Teruko K. Chin. May 1979.

18. Japanese economy and politics: selected serial titles. By Teruko K. Chin. Feb. 1980.

WASHINGTON UNIVERSITY
in St. Louis

East Asian Library

Washington University in St. Louis, East Asian Library
Established in 1964
St. Louis, Missouri 63130

I. Background
Faculty: 8
Enrollment for Asian Studies: an average of 40, 78% graduates

II. Organization
1. Location: January Hall (Former Law School Building)
2. Holdings:
    a) <u>Monographs</u>: 41,876 volumes, including 67 uncataloged current imprints, representing 13,215 cataloged titles.

    Major subject distribution in percentages:
    Hist. = 25%   Lang. & Lit.= 35%   Soc. Sci. = 17%

L.C. Classification	Titles
General works, Bibliography	769
Philosophy	293
Religion	800
History	2,888
Japanese History, 1,877	
Geography	370
Social Science, Economics, Sociology	1,497
Political Science, Law	488
Education	298
Music	34
Fine Arts	923
Language & Literature	4,570
Japanese Language, 421	
Japanese Literature, 3,601	
Science & Technology	146
Military Science	139
Total	13,215

    b) <u>Microfilm</u>: 0
    c) <u>Periodical subscriptions</u>: 146 titles
    d) <u>Newspapers</u>: 2 titles
3. Staff: .5 academic (Head, East Asian Library), 1 non-academic, 37 hours/week student help. Head reports to Dean of Library Services.

III. Collection Management
1. Classification system: L.C. and H-Y
2. Shelving of books: separately by language
3. Public catalog: author, title and subject in alphabetical order, separately by language
4. Book selection: Head, East Asian Library and requests from professors

5. Acquisitions:
   1973-78 (five years)   5,756 volumes
   1978-79   540 volumes
   Periodicals/subscriptions   146 titles
6. Cataloging: 1977-78
   Monographs   315 titles
   Added volumes   283 volumes
   By L.C. cards   172 titles
   Original cataloging   143 titles
   Recataloged (class change)   780 volumes
7. Circulation: Open hours: M - F, 8:30 am - 10 pm; Sa - Su, 1 pm - 6 pm
   Sample circulation figures: 9/78-12/78 (four months)
      Total: 1,157 volumes
      Subject distribution: History, 9%; Language and Literature, 69%; Art, 10%; Religion and Philosophy, 7%; Social Sciences, 4%.
8. Financing:
   a) <u>Book budget</u>: 1979-80
      University Library fund, monographs $4,500
      University Library fund, paid serials   6,000
      Outside funds   8,000
      Total $18,500

   Average price of subscription: $38 per title
   Average price of monograph: $13 per volume

   b) <u>Salaries</u>: Total for 1.5 staff and students, $22,570
   c) <u>Other expenses</u>: covered by General Library, including travel, which is partially reimbursed by General Library.

Washington University in St. Louis   Nov., 1979, Revised Jan., 1980

Washington University in St. Louis, founded in 1853, is a private, nondenominational university. William G. Eliot, the first President of the Board of Directors and third Chancellor, and the grandfather of the poet T.S. Eliot, was instrumental in having the University named in honor of George Washington, the first institution of higher education to bear the name. John M. Olin Library, the main library, was opened in 1962 to replace the old one. Two years later, with its modest beginnings, the East Asian Collection was organized and housed on the fifth floor of Olin Library. In 1972, when the Law School Library was relocated to a new building, its facilities were made available to the East Asian Library—three levels of books stacks, a large reading room, and an office area.

The East Asian Library held in 1979, a collectin of about 92,000 volumes in Chinese and Japanese. It is the Olin Library that houses most of the Western materials on Asia. Within the library structure, the East Asian Library is one of the departmental and school libraries, and its head reports directly to the Dean of Library Services—the head of the entire library system. The Japanese collection of some 41,000 volumes serves primarily the Japanese Studies program on campus. In recent years, it has also enjoyed strong support from the Art and Archaeology Department, which is locally endowed. The Art Library has an impressive East Asian art collection, for which the East Asian Library handles the acquisitions of books and cataloging.

With its imposing size, the reading room not only provides reference services for the East Asian Library, but also serves as a study hall for students from other disciplines—the environment with long wooden tables, leaded windows with red curtains, and an arching ceiling, is often compared by students and visitors to that of Oxford. Here the reference books and current journals are kept for easy access, as is the card catalog that records the library holdings by author, title, and subject in alphabetical order.

UNIVERSITY OF WISCONSIN

East Asian Collection

University of Wisconsin Memorial Library, East Asian Collection
Established in 1960
Madison, Wisconsin 53706

I. Background
Faculty: 9
Enrollment: figures not available

II. Organization
1. Location: Second floor of the main library
2. Holdings:
    a) <u>Monographs:</u> 31,671 volumes, including 200 uncataloged monographs, representing 17,360 cataloged titles.

    Major subject distribution in percentages:
    Hist. = 32%   Lang. & Lit.= 44%   Soc. Sci. = 9%

L.C. Classification	Titles
General works	110
Philosophy	240
Religion (Buddhism, 495)	1,100
History	5,410
Japanese History, 4,205	
Geography	200
Social Science, Economics, Sociology	1,280
Political Science	150
Law	30
Education	165
Music	162
Fine Arts	350
Language & Literature	7,613
Japanese Language and Literature, 7,455	
Science & Technology	140
Military Science	210
Bibliography	200
Total	17,360

    b) <u>Microfilm:</u> 45 titles on 50 reels
    c) <u>Periodical subscriptions:</u> 193 titles
    d) <u>Newspapers:</u> 5 titles
3. Staff: No Japanese staff, 3 Chinese professionals. Bibliographer reports to Chief of Reference Services; catalogers report to Head of the Cataloging Department.

III. Collection Management
1. Classification system: L.C.
2. Shelving of books: intershelved with main library holdings
3. Public catalog: East Asian cards interfiled in public catalog of the main library; separate catalog of Japanese and Chinese books in the East Asian reading room.

4. Book selection: East Asian bibliographer, blanket order to Japan Publications Trading Co., and recommendations of faculty.
5. Acquisitions:
1973	2,110 volumes
1974-75	2,100 volumes
1976-77	no record
1977-78	2,516 volumes
6. Cataloging: 1977-78
Number of titles cataloged	531
Added volumes	155
By L.C. cards	160 titles
Original cataloging	272 titles
Recataloging	99 titles
7. Circulation: Open hours: M - F, 8 am - Midnight; Su, Noon - 9 pm. Circulation figures not available.
8. Financing: 1977-78
   a) <u>Book budget</u>:
   University funds for East Asian books ($36,000) include an estimated one-third for Japanese books
Japanese books (est.)	$12,000
Subscriptions, periodicals, serials, continuations (est.)	4,800
Estimated total	$16,800

   Average price of books: $25 per volume (estimate)

   b) <u>Salaries</u>: 3 non-Japanese professionals are committed to spend a percentage of their time working with Japanese materials.

University of Wisconsin Memorial Library   July, 1979, Revised April, 1980

The Japanese collection, a part of the East Asia collection, is under the general supervision of Dr. Chester Wang, one of the eight area bibliographers of the library system. In 1978 the undergraduate reading room was moved and its former quarters were made into the East Asia Reading Room. There is extensive space along the walls for shelving reference books. However, the major portion of the books are shelved in the stacks along with the main library books, dispersed according to the classifications.

The work of the East Asia bibliographer involves selecting books and giving references, and reporting to the Chief of the Reference Services. He is not immediately responsible for catalogers, who work under the Catalog Department. Acquisition and serial work is done by staff members of the respective sections. There is a separate catalog of Chinese and Japanese books in the Reading Room, whose cards are duplicated in the general catalog. The shelf list, however, is not duplicated. Thus, the main shelf list is the only source of information given by subject classification.

There are plans for a separate stack and a reading room for the East Asia Collection when an annex building is completed at some future date. Until then, it is rather difficult to determine the present state of the Japanese collection. Dr. Chester Wang is a student of Japanese literature, but there is no native Japanese staff member working in the library.

The book budget for the East Asia area is estimated at 8 percent of the total book budget of the University Library. One percent is approximately $3,000 - $4,000, depending on the capital allocation for the year. A blanket order of $1,621 per year is made with the Japan Publications Trading Company.

YALE UNIVERSITY

East Asian Collection

Yale University, East Asian Collection
Established in 1878
120 High Street, New Haven, Connecticut 06520

I. Background
Faculty: 16
Graduate students: 105 (27 master's and 3 doctoral degrees awarded in June 1980)
Undergraduates: 57 in first year Japanese language course in Fall 1980

II. Organization
1. Location: Sterling Memorial Library
2. Holdings: 1980
   a) <u>Monographs</u>: 119,232 volumes, including 2,050 uncataloged materials, representing 49,667 cataloged titles

   <u>Major subject distribution in percentages:</u>
   Hist. = 35%   Lang. & Lit.= 24%   Soc. Sci. = 20%

L.C. Classification, plus H-Y Classification, plus Yale Classification	Titles
General works	1,019
Philosophy, Religion	3,709
Buddhism, 1,374	
History	15,948
Japanese History, 11,087	
Geography	1,299
Social Science, Economics, Sociology	6,795
Political Science	1,857
Law	301
Education	1,202
Music	411
Fine Arts	1,714
Language & Literature	12,119
Japanese Language and Literature, 9,856	
Science & Technology	1,640
Military Science	613
Bibliography	1,040
Total	49,667

   b) <u>Microfilm</u>: 4,609 reels (both Chinese and Japanese)
   c) <u>Periodical subscriptions</u>: 863 items (annuals included), with 583 paid and 280 through gifts and exchange.
   d) <u>Newspapers</u>: 2 titles by air

3. Staff: 3.75 professionals, 4.75 technical and clericals, .6 student help. Head of the East Asian collection reports to University Librarian.

III. Collection Management
1. Classification system: L.C., H-Y, and Yale
2. Shelving of books: intershelved with main library holdings by subject
3. Public catalog: interfiled in main public catalog. Separate catalog for East Asian languages, maintained in East Asia catalog room.
4. Book selection: East Asian Collection Curator
5. Acquisitions:
   - 1973-78 31,089 volumes, including bound periodicals counted as one volume to each title
   - 1978-79 4,480 volumes, including 53 new serial subscriptions
6. Cataloging: 1978-79

Total	4,817 titles
By L.C. cards (82%)	3,969 titles
Original cataloging (18%)	858 titles

7. Circulation: Open hours (East Asian Collection reading room): M - Th, 8:30 am - 10 pm; F, 8:30 am - 5 pm; Sa, 10 am - 5 pm; Su, 2 pm - 10 pm. New England area scholars are given free admittance to stacks, paid by HEW grant (fee is $15/month for outside borrowing privileges).
   No sample circulation figures available.
8. Financing:
   a) <u>Book budget:</u>

Year	Source	EAC	Japan
1977-78	Library	$68,660	One-half
	HEW	25,000	of
	Mellon	17,590	EAC
	Sumitomo	40,000	total
	Total	$158,750	
1978-79	Library	$107,410	One-half
	HEW	31,482	of
	Mellon	4,198	EAC
	JUSFC	30,655	total
	Total	$173,745	
1979-80	Library	$88,895	$44,448
	HEW	37,500	
	JUSFC	3,798	
	Outside	17,500	37,248
	Total	$147,693	$81,696

   b) <u>Salaries:</u> Total for 8.5 staff and .6 student, $117,172 (1979-80)
   c) <u>Operating budget:</u>

Maintenance & repairs of office machines	$225
Business travel (professional travel through Central budget)	671
Copying, administrative	150
Postage (other than letters) & supplies	1,110
Telephone	200
Equipment budget (from Central budget)	0
Total	$2,356

Yale University   Dec., 1979, Revised Aug., 1980

The Yale University Library has an arrangement for its East Asian Collection which is unique among major East Asian collections in the country. Books are arranged on shelves according to subject classifications regardless of what language they are written in. One might say that it is ideal for a research library, but perhaps impractical at times. The Japanese books are no exception, and are dispersed according to the classifications among the 3,805,199 holdings kept in the Sterling Memorial Library. Access to these books is controlled by the Main public catalog, containing author, title, and subject cards. A separate author, title and subject catalog for East Asian languages—Chinese, Japanese, and Korean—is maintained in the East Asia catalog room. Besides this, there is a classified catalog for each language, in which the completed catalog cards are filed. This, however, is not a shelf list in the strict sense, because there is a time lag of up to one year in some cases, from the time books are cataloged until their printed cards are returned for filing. So the official shelf list remains with the Main Library's shelf list.

Bookplates on Japanese books in the collection reveal some of the early gifts to Yale. For instance, a substantial number of pre-Meiji books were donated by O.C. Marsh, Yale Professor of Paleontology and a connoisseur of Oriental artifacts in 1873. In 1884, Professor Frederick Wells Williams presented his alma mater with the books collected by his father, Professor S. Wells Williams. However, more systematic acquisition began with the effort of Professor Kan'ichi Asakawa, the first curator of the East Asian Collection and a noted scholar on feudalism, who collected materials for Yale and the Library of Congress during his stay in Japan in 1906-1907.

The collection has also been enriched by the acquisition of such special materials as those in the Yale Association of Japan collection, which is now housed in the Beinecke Rare Book and Manuscript Library. This gift colletion of some 350 items and many more pieces was presented to Yale in 1934. With a fund raised by Yale alumni in the Tokyo area, Professor Katsumi Kuroita of Tokyo Imperial University was commissioned to select and acquire this special collections of books, manuscripts, and other articles of literary, artistic and historical interest to illustrate the culture and civilization of old Japan. Some original documents in the collection date as far back as the 11th century, while the earliest Buddhist sutras (Chinese version), in manuscript and printed form, are from 8th century Japan. Professor Asakawa, who laid the foundation of the collection and devised the Yale Classification system for its materials, donated some 3,700 volumes that were collected for his research on feudalism in 1943.

Responding to the needs of the growing East Asian Studies program at Yale in recent years, the acquisition of research materials directly in support of the program was made the primary objective. In order to cope with the fast growing collection, especially after World War II, the successive curators adopted the Harvard-Yenching system, modified for Yale, and finally, during the 1960-70's, changed to the Library of Congress classification system for new acquisitions, allowing only minimal recataloging of old books. In the 1960's, the General Library, having acquired storage space, decided to retire books in less frequent use, and formulated an elaborate policy statement for retirement. Accordingly, books were put into Retirement Storage, but one catalog card was left in the Main Public Catalog. Thus, one central bibliographic control keeps the library materials accessible to all users regardless of the locations of books in the stacks or in different classification systems.

The administrative operation is conducted by the East Asian Collection curator who reports to the University Librarian. He is responsible for personnel matters, book funds, office expenses, book selection, technical and reference services, etc., and is expected to supervise this intangible collection of East Asian language books.

Some users and area scholars find this situation of dispersed books inconvenient, perhaps because they must exert extra leg work to use it. However, where the East Asia Collection in other universities is "independent" or "segregated" from the Main Library, the situation found at Yale presents a workable alternative system. The Japanese books, as well as other non-Western language books, are available to anyone using the resources in the stacks and in the Public Catalog. It seems the system is well integrated into the University Library so that a good rapport exists between the Main Library administration and the East Asia Collection.

Bibliography

Hahn, Bokson. 1965. A study of East Asian Library at Yale University: History, Collection, Services. M.A. thesis, Yale University.

Publications

Catalogue of books, manuscripts and other articles of literary, artistic and historical interest, illustrative of the culture and civilization of old Japan, presented to Yale University, U.S.A. by the Yale association of Japan, Tokyo. (Tokyo, Taiheiyosha press, 1934) 4 v. in 1. (The books were selected by a historian, Dr. Katsumi Kuroita of Tokyo University.)

Gifts of the Yale Association of Japan. Prepared by K. Asakawa. 1945. 143 sheets. (Adds a few more titles to the above mentioned 1934 Tokyo edition.)

East Asia Collection Annual reports.

Access to the East Asia Collection. By Hideo Kaneko, curator. 1979. 3 typed sheets.

Yale University Library - Facts. 1978. Pamphlet.

Yale University Library - Library privileges. 1976. Pamphlet.

OBSERVATIONS AND ISSUES

Observations and Issues

Dr. Tsuen-Hsiun Tsien, former director of Far Eastern Library, University of Chicago, describes in detail the development of East Asian Libraries in the United States in his report: Current Status of East Asian Collections in American Libraries, 1974/75 (published by Center for Chinese Research Materials and Association of Research Libraries, Washington, D.C., 1976. 67p.) It covers 93 collections which hold Chinese, Japanese, and Korean materials.

Since the present survey covers only 28 of those collections, the conclusions drawn here are necessarily limited in scope. The collections surveyed, however, include all of the major Japanese holdings in the United States; their strength and problems can be taken as indicative of those of other libraries as well.

The general survey of 28 research libraries in the United States—Library of Congress and 27 university libraries—each of which holds over 10,000 volumes of Japanese materials, revealed the following:

Total number of holdings:	2,381,422	vols.	100%
Library of Congress	666,816	vols.	28%
27 university libraries	1,714,606	vols.	72%
Cataloged items	1,881,317	vols.	79%
Uncataloged items (including about 10,000 current publications)	500,105	vols.	21%
Holdings in titles (an average of 2.2 volumes per title	850,328	titles	

Included in this uncataloged group are pre-Meiji books in their Japanese bindings, pre-war publications, some of them outdated by newer publications, incomplete periodical numbers, miscellaneous pamphlets and pamphlet series which do not require immediate processing, duplicates, etc. Some 68 percent of this group, 340,000 items, are in the Library of Congress and are now being sorted. All these "uncataloged" items are listed briefly so that they are available on request by users. Thus, at present 1,881,317 volumes, representing 850,328 titles, are fully cataloged and accessible through public catalogs.

Major Subject Distribution by Regions (in titles)

U.S. Regions	Phil/Rel	History	Lang & Lit	Soc. Sci.
East, Lib. of Congress	39,841	110,117	109,151	131,509
Midwest, Texas	12,600	48,057	53,578	37,208
West	12,964	38,030	36,250	52,918
Hawaii	2,845	6,383	6,603	5,495
Total	68,250	202,587	205,582	227,130
	10%	29%	29%	32%

This table demonstrates that the principal repositories for Japanese materials are in the eastern United States, primarily because that region includes the Library of Congress and four university libraries each holding over 70,000 volumes. The particular strength of social sciences holding in the west can be attributed to the Hoover Institution collection at Stanford.

Financing

Book Budgets:
Library of Congress (subscriptions excluded)	⁺156,319	13%
27 university libraries (subs. included)	1,080,522	87%
Total	$1,236,841	100%

Average price per volume: Library of Congress $13.00
                            27 University Libraries $20.00

University libraries include periodical subscriptions and mailing costs in book funds, while the Library of Congress uses Army postal arrangements, which cost approximately $25,000 annually.

Salaries:
   Library of Congress: $962,290 (base pay scale) for 43.5 staff members, an average of $22,122.
   27 University Libraries: $1,362,193 (current payment) for 89.7 staff members, an average of $15,186.

Categories of libraries:

While libraries all serve to provide Japanese materials to faculty members and students, variations in their size and situation create different problems in program development and operation management. The survey includes the Japanese collection at the Library of Congress, with its 666,000 volumes, which bears little comparison with the other Japanese collections. At the other end of the scale, there are eight university libraries with holdings of 10,000 to 40,000 volumes which are administered by only one professional librarian, assisted by a few clericals. As a result some libraries have an immediate necessary interest in finding ways for one person to handle collection development, public service, bibliographical work, and administrative functions. Larger libraries with their more specialized staff and more systematic organization are often concerned with coordinating and articulating new and operating programs; these libraries have an interest in general plans for maintaining and improving services, sometimes in the face of reduced budgets. To distinguish them, the university collections in this survey have been grouped, by the number of volumes they hold, into three categories, and the Library of Congress is given a separate entry. (See Table V, General Status of Libraries by ˜izes)

Two collections examined, that at the Claremont College Library, with 10,000 volumes, and at Northwestern University Library with 20,000, are inactive at present and have been omitted from the final calculations. Claremont's collection contains more books on religion than on other subjects, while Northwestern's collection emphasizes pre-war publications on Japanese law and politics. Summary descriptions of the library programs of the three groups follows.

Group I (over 60,000 volumes): Programs within the host universities cover academic as well as professional disciplines, and curricula provide for undergraduate and graduate degrees. The libraries in this group are expected to be prepared to assist their clientele with bibliograhical information at all levels of research, from standard instructional books to archival source materials.

Group II (20,000-60,000 volumes): The programs supported by the libraries in this group are not as extensive as with Group I; most Group II programs were started during the 1960s. The libraries have collected instructional materials for courses offered and research materials on selected subjects needed by graduate students and faculty members.

Group III (10,000-20,000 volumes): Program emphasis here is on language and literature. Other disciplines such as history, politics, etc., are mostly treated within undergraduate courses. The libraries in this group are operated by one professional, sometimes working only on a part-time basis. Books and periodicals are acquired largely to meet the demands of faculty members for teaching and for keeping up with their research.

Funding by Groups (1979-80 averages)

	University Funds	Outside Funds	Total
Group I	$46,574	$24,576	$71,150
Group II	18,305	3,182	21,487
Group III	10,606	300	10,906

Acquisitions (annual averages)

Group I	4,069
Group II	1,338
Group III	727

Collection Management:

Collection building:[1] Professional librarians understand that building good collections demands acquiring not only numbers of books in various subjects, but also books which reflect the needs of library users. Since money for personnel, books, and facilities is scarce, libraries are compelled to balance aspirations against funding realities. That this may lead to hardheaded evaluation of their collections and services can be a benefit, however, especially if evaluations uncover ways to meet users' needs more effectively. Programs facilitating interlibrary loans and coordinating book purchases with other institutions in the region may greatly increase the utility of collections without much increasing costs. It is time for collections to be studied in the context of the national library community, to conduct quantitative and especially qualitative evaluations, and to define realistic policies for collection building. Evaluations should reflect the needs of Japanese studies programs at each institution and the uses made of the existing collection, setting priorities in book purchasing by type of book (reference books, archival source materials, scholarly treatises, and standard works constituting a core collection) as well as by importance and subject. (cp.: "University of Kansas, East Asian Studies." p. 78)

The regional consortiums established in 1978 with funding from the Japan-U.S. Friendship Commission to coordinate library services and book purchase among ten major U.S. university libraries are clearly a step in the right direction. But continued funding and an extension of the program to incorporate small and medium-sized Japanese collections are essential if the consortiums are to fulfill their mission.

2) Core Collection: There are guides to reference books and subject bibliographies published in recent years, but no list of standard books on all subjects are available. In the 1950's, the University of Michigan, Center for Japanese Studies published a bibliograhical series of guides to reference and research under ten subjects. Japanese collections which came into being in the following decades used them for book selection. The political science volume was updated in 1960, geography in 1970, and in 1970 a sociology and social anthropology volume was added. The bibliography on history which

---

[1] Collection Development policies and practice. Sponsored by Association of College and Research Libraries. Published by ALA, 1980. 2 cassettes

covered a wide range of subject survey histories has not been updated since its publication in 1954. The gap of some twenty-six years has left the libraries without this special source for selecting books or evaluating their collections. It will be very useful if this bibliography is brought up-to-date and be kept up-to-date by some means with cooperation of Japanese librarians, perhaps through the planned bibliography of reference books by the Sub-Committee on Japanese Materials under the Committee on East Asian Libraries (CEAL), or through a timely combined bibliography of reference works and standard books.

3) <u>Records of uses:</u>[2] The uses made of the existing collection are also a means of evaluation. This survey does not, or could not, find data on Japanese collection circulation from libraries who handle it through the General Library Circulation Desk. However, even in the absence of circulation records, a librarian may still evaluate collections-utility by checking what books have been used in the reading room areas, or by which books professors assign students to read. A good rapport between users and librarians helps librarians in selecting books of probable importance. Libraries contributing their circulation records to this survey spent a good deal of time to do so; such records, however, provide crucial information about library use and can be an effective basis for a rational acquisitions policy. Such data can be acquired simply through a sample survey covering peak circulation months or a term.

4) <u>Library services:</u> Libraries have ways to encourage use of their collections such as (1) by circulating information about new acquisitions or sometimes (2) by informing specialist researchers about specific articles found in current periodicals, (3) by providing easy access to collections by filing analytical cards of big sets of collected works in the public catalog (which saves time for both users and librarians) or (4) by providing personal assistance, participating in classroom teaching or assisting in curriculum development through bibliograhical reference services. A librarian's familiarity with book usage, especially if it is supported by circulation figures, is a good guide in enlarging certain areas within a collection. The usefulness of a good collection can also be augmented if librarians are able to provide information on the location of books in other libraries in the United States, or to provide links to professional contacts and access to special collections in Japan. A specialist who is to visit Japan to do research needs to be well prepared so that his/her precious time may be used to its best advantage.

---

[2] <u>Measuring the circulation use of a small academic library collection: A manual.</u> Associated colleges of the Midwest. To be published by the Office of Management Studies, Association of Research Libraries in 1981. This gives a step by step procedure and how to use the results.

5) <u>Funding</u>: According to the <u>Japan Publisher's Yearbook, 1980</u>, p.1289, the number of books being published has increased steadily over the last ten years; in 1979 there were 27,177 new monographs selling for an average price of Y2,483 (about $10.00), and 3,160 periodicals. Going over the trade lists title by title, a rough estimate of books whose content would relate to Japanese studies come to between 6,000 and 7,000 titles. Such a list would include certain important government publications placed on public sale. The National Diet Library, which is a depository of Japanese government documents, received 10,711 monographs in 1978, including 5,023 central government, 4,945 local government, and 803 national and public university publications, and 4,038 periodical titles. These figures represented about 75 percent of the total government publications, and of this 75 percent, the Library of Congress received 59 percent, or 6,342 items, of the monographs, and 39 percent, or 1,545 items, of the periodicals. The University of California at Berkeley—the second largest depository in the United States—received 799 monographs and 252 periodicals.

In 1979 the Library of Congress budgeted $150,000 for the purchase of Japanese monographs. With this money, 7,501 titles in 9,439 volumes were acquired. Periodical subscriptions are purchased from the Serials Department budget and a separate figure is not available for Japanese periodicals. Besides trade books, the Library received over 6,342 government monographic titles. The number of books university libraries purchase per annum is about 4,000-5,000 at the most, and this figure includes government publications. (See Table 2)

What constitutes an adequate yearly acquisition of new books depends on different criteria at each library. Those preparing long range plans for source materials acquisition with respect to their probable funding may be able to use this survey and statistical tables. For the present it is important to note that the enormous collection and immeasurable services available from the Library of Congress assist individual scholars and libraries not only in the United States but also all over the world. Still, at times certain scholarly books can be found only in the collections of university libraries. Library book selection is therefore an important problem and pooling information concerning it vital.

a) Institutional support for funding: The primary funding for purchasing books rests with the host university library, supported by the institutional program center. Its place in the general library's itemized book budget was the official source which this survey depended on for funding data. Librarians should be prepared to turn first to the university library for necessary funding; to be most effective, they should present well researched figures on their collection, its uses by the university community, and its needs. Comparative data, relying on information about other collections and presented persuasively, may help convince the faculty and the library administration to support requested funding if the situation permits.

b) Endowment and foundation support: In the 1960's libraries had to expand the subject coverage of Japanese collections to accomodate fast-growing Japanese studies programs. Recognizing this increased activity, the United States government through the National Defense Education Act included library funds in their East Asia area studies program support. In 1973 the Japan Foundation made extensive funds available to ten American universities and their libraries. The money for libraries was badly needed in areas required by new programs. In addition, the Ford Foundation and later, the Mellon Foundation gave funds including the library support. In 1978 the Japan-U.S. Friendship Commission started to help the ten libraries by supplementing purchasing funds which had not been able to keep with inflated book costs, especially for those published in Japan. Their gifts to the already established large collections was to enable them to maintain their usefulness with the condition that the receipient libraries try not to duplicate expensive acquisitions or materials destined for infrequent use, such as big sets of source materials, and further, to coordinate their future acquisitions in specialized fields. To fulfill this condition, the libraries formed regional consortiums: Havard-Yenching, Yale, Princeton, and Columbia in the East; Chicago and Michigan in the Midwest; and the University of California at Berkeley and Hoover in the West; leaving the University of Washington (Seattle) and Hawaii as self-sustaining. The consortiums were also intended to promote coordination and cooperation between libraries within their respective regions.

These gifts created considerable discussion among libraries which were not direct recipients, but which also needed extra funds to develop their collections. The Japan Foundation and some private foundations came to the support of these libraries with extra funds, but long-range plans based on better cooperation and sharing among all groups of libraries need to be developed.

To promote a better understanding of the situation, the Japan-U.S. Friendship Commission sponsored a workshop in 1978, coordinated by the Association of Research Libraries, Office of Management Studies, directed by Duane E. Webster. The results were summarized in Workshop for Japanese Collection Librarians in American Research Libraries (August 28-30, 1978. 111, 34p.). As a follow-up project, Dr. Shizue Matsuda of Indiana University compiled and published Current Japanese Serials in the Humanities and Social Sciences in American Libraries (Indiana University Library, East Asian Collection, 1980. 337p.). Another project is this survey of Japanese collections.

Positions in the university library organization:

As mentioned in the introduction, Japanese studies programs were mostly started in the post-war period to remedy the neglect of area studies. In the 35 years since the end of the war, these programs have spread to many universities and colleges and to various educational levels. However, predictions for the 1980's are eloquently summed up in the following article, "East Asian characters: Ending the silence" (The Research Libraries Group News. Issue no. 2, September, 1980. p.5)

> Unfortunately, according to careful analyses of the field made in recent studies, East Asian libraries cannot look forward to the kind of growth seen in the recent past. Many collections have already begun to cut back on new acquisitions, and some libraries have been forced to reduce reference support and other reader services. Rapidly rising costs and diminishing possibilities for financial support are making institutional autonomy an impossible dream from a bygone age.
>
> The problem is one shared by all research institutions—shrinking budgets on the one hand, increased user demand on the other. A 1977 report issued by the American Council of Learned Societies warns:
>
> "It is evident that our institutions of higher education can no longer continue to develop autonomous East Asian research libraries of expensive and relatively infrequenly used research resources in the face of rapidly escalating costs, exponential growth in the literature, and stable or declining prospects for the fiscal support of these collections.
>
> "At the same time it is clearly very much in the national interest to have effective scholarly access to the very large bodies of current and retrospective material required for the study of East Asia."
>
> Their answer to the problem is shared resources, and to accomlish the mammoth task of developing a workable network, "a comprehensive East Asian bibliograhic data base, one that can be made widely and quickly available to a large and growing number of interested scholars and institutions throughout the country, must be established. This is a basic and absolutely essential requirement for the shared use of resources."

The age of computer cataloging East Asian language materials is approaching in a few years, the target date being 1983/84 according to the article. The situation calls for a positive approach to problems common to all East Asian libraries. There are many questions to be answered before computer cataloging systems can take over daily library chores; even after a it, etc. are only a few of the problems which each library must solve. For some libraries the change may not be so great as for others; but once automation is adopted, it is here to stay and is bound to influence both technical and service procedures of library work. Except for original cataloging, most of the routine cataloging may then be done by computer staff who have little knowledge of the East Asian languages. Acquisitions through blanket orders to dealers may become a possibility. In small East Asian units some staff members who have hitherto enjoyed stable status as specialists may find themselves relocated. Under automated bibliographic information services, subject or area specialists will be expected to give broader and/or more specific information, to interpret items on computer-generated bibliographies, or to compile bibliographies needed by research scholars and for classroom use. In other words specialists may be called on as interpreters and experts on the native culture, not only to build collections.

At present, East Asian Library committees of the Research Library Group, the Association of Research Libraries, and CEAL in the Association for Asian Studies are studying ways of improving collections, their uses, and services from various directions: technical, operation management, funding, etc., on a national basis. Still any nation-wide planning must understand that collections vary in their development, and that it is difficult to help all equally or to spend the available funds selectively in the most effective and economical way. Once a decision is made it is up to the recipients to find the best way to share the benefit with others. Toward this end in recent years more interlibrary loans have been reported by various libraries. The establishment of a center for East Asian archival source materials, previous runs of periodicals, microforms, little used materials, and science and technology, in the Center for Research Libraries in Chicago is encouraging to all concerned. Development in computerized cataloging now under study by Research Libraries Group/Research Libraries Information Network will also bring about changes in librarianship. However, underlying all these factors, the well-being of an individual library depends on good friendly relations among librarians. It is an important factor for any plan to be successful. It will be a challenge to all if some definite system is worked out in which they can participate, or a continuous project planned to which they can contribute for the benefit of all.

APPENDICES

APPENDIX I:
Japanese Collection Resources of U.S. Libraries (holdings over 10,000 volumes)

University (Year of Survey)	No. of Volumes 1978-79 (*1980)	Precats. (vols.)	No. of Titles	Major Subjects (%) Hist.	L. & L.	S.Sci.	Circulation (samples)	No. of Faculty
Arizona (79)	23,125*	2,000	7,675	24	27	19		6
UC Berkeley (80)	189,575	42,702	54,570	22	23	29	983 (6 mos.) Japanese	28
UCLA (79)	71,200	7,000	15,353	25	27	21	2,136 (4 mos., 1977) Oriental	13
UC Santa Barbara (80)	22,115	604	6,494	28	29	24		5
Chicago (80)	89,485	1,337	42,455	25	28	24	1,518 (Fall, 1979) EA	13
Claremont (79)	10,000							1
Columbia (80)	156,693	27,471	64,975	29	21	25	855 (July, 1980) Japanese	25
Cornell (79)	32,900	0	15,654	24	34	17	625v. (4 mos.)	7
Harvard-Yenching (79) Harvard Law Harvard Fine Arts Total	154,368 13,000 5,000 172,368	1,000	86,222 7,482 (4,000)	23	24	24	3,601v. (1980, 4 mos.) Japanese	27 4
Hawaii (79)	78,793*	12,412	23,121	28	29	24	24,977 (78-79) Asia Library	87

University (Year of Survey)	No. of Volumes 1978-79 (*1980)	Precats. (vols.)	No. of Titles	Major Subjects (%) Hist.	L. & L.	S.Sci.	Circulation (samples)	No. of Faculty
Hoover (79) Fine Arts Total	101,598 487 102,085	7,500	53,694	21	15	48	1,376 (4. mos. 1978) Japanese, including in-house use	25
Illinois (79)	35,000	3,000	15,250	26	30	25	4,350 (78-79) East Asia	13
Indiana (79) Indiana Fine Arts Total	23,790 498 24,288	500	8,957	28	38	12		9
Kansas (79)	29,000	10,000[a]	5,826	28	23	32	1,690 (78-79) East Asia (75-76)	10
Maryland (80)	52,787	25,000	20,837	25	37	20	204 (6 mos., 1979) Japanese; 1,641 periodicals, EA	7
Michigan (79) Michigan Law Total	148,838 9,300 158,138	4,750[a] 1,300 6,050	53,492	30	25	25	815 (4 mos., 1979) Japanese 8,733 (79-80) EA	20
Minnesota (80)	18,290	200	6,200	22	45	17		9
Northwestern (75)	13,163							
Ohio State (79)	12,476	2,000	3,342	21	56	12		8
Oregon (79)	15,634	234	5,352	23	30	11		6
Pennsylvania (80)	25,000	1,600	7,219	26	41	12		5

University (Year of Survey)	No. of Volumes 1978-79 (*1980)	Precats. (vols.)	No. of Titles	Major Subjects (%) Hist.	L. & L.	S.Sci.	Circulation (samples)	No. of Faculty
Pittsburgh (79)	13,000	750	4,301	43	20	23		6
Princeton (80)	70,774	410	29,771	28	27	24	2,299 (6 mos., 1979) EA	11
Rochester (79)	10,894	18	4,873	28	30	12	10,400 (1977-1978) EA	5
Texas (79)	28,994	2,000	7,085	29	35	23		7
Univ. of Washington Law School Total	59,700 30,000 89,700	4,000	20,400	27	28	21	2,595 (3 mos., 1978) EA	19
Washington University	41,876	67	13,215	25	35	17	1,157 (4 mos., 1979) EA	8
Wisconsin (79)	31,671	200	17,360	32	44	9		9
Yale (79)	119,232*	2,050[a]	49,667[b]	35	24	20		16
Library of Congress (80) Law Library Total	606,816 60,000 666,816	340,000	195,486 18,036 213,522	17	20	35	1,700v./mo.	
Totals (excluding Claremont and Northwestern)	2,381,422v.	500,105v.	850,328t.					

a. Principally items for recataloging. b. 1978-79; 1 year behind in filing shelf list cards.

APPENDIX II:
Average Annual Growth of Collections, 1975-1979
(Number of Volumes)

Library	1975 Holdings	1979 Holdings	4 or 5 Year Increase	Average Annual Increase
Lib. of Congress	545,661	606,816	61,155	12,231
Arizona	31,462	23,125		
Berkeley	170,005	189,575	19,570	4,892
UCLA	66,000	71,200	5,200	1,300
UC-Santa Barbara	13,619	22,115	8,496	1,699
Chicago	67,918	89,485	21,567	4,313
Columbia	135,636	156,693	21,057	4,211
Cornell	30,471	32,900	2,429	607
Harvard-Yenching	138,450	154,368	15,918	3,979
Hawaii	65,946	78,793	12,847	2,569
Hoover	78,562	101,598	23,036	4,607
Illinois	30,342	35,000	4,658	1,165
Indiana	15,908	23,790	7,882	1,970
Kansas	23,786	29,000	5,214	1,304
Maryland	83,638	52,787		
Michigan	128,382	148,838	20,456	4,773
Minnesota	15,691	18,290	2,599	520
Ohio State	9,383	12,476	3,093	773
Oregon	11,650	15,634	3,984	996
Pennsylvania	24,063	25,000	937	187
Pittsburgh	7,845	13,000	5,155	1,289
Princeton	52,336	70,774	18,438	4,610
Rochester	10,659	10,894	235	59
Texas	22,329	28,994	6,665	1,904
Washington—Seattle	45,494	59,700	14,206	3,556
Law Library	28,000	30,000	2,000	400
Washington—St.Louis	32,798	41,876	9,078	2,269
Wisconsin	33,090	31,671		
Yale	91,505	119,232	27,727	5,545
27 University Library Total		1,714,606	262,447	52,489
Plus Library of Congress				
Grand Total		**2,381,422**		

APPENDIX III:
Funding 1979-80, Book Budget

Library	Budget	University Funding	Outside Funding
Arizona	$31,200	$26,200	$5,000
Berkeley	95,102	58,346	36,756
UCLA	27,989	19,798	8,191
UC-Santa Barbara	18,000	18,000	
Chicago[b]	58,125	19,265	38,860
Columbia[b]	81,513	59,915	21,598
Cornell[b]	29,398	22,398	7,000
Harvard-Yenching	79,311		79,311
Hawaii	49,835	47,035	2,800
Hoover	62,781	57,781	5,000
Illinois[b]	42,000	32,000	10,000
Indiana	22,142	10,142	12,000
Kansas[b]	18,987	18,987	
Maryland	19,019	19,019	
Michigan	102,500	50,000	52,000
Minnesota	12,380	12,380	
Ohio State	10,142	10,142	
Oregon[b]	13,170	11,670	1,500
Pennsylvania	13,000	13,000	
Pittsburgh[a]	16,337	16,337	
Princeton	75,960	34,750	41,210
Rochester	2,500+	2,500+	
Texas	14,307	14,307	
Washington—Seattle	54,628	28,508	26,120
Law Library	13,150	13,150	
Washington—St.Louis	18,500	10,500	8,000
Wisconsin[a]	16,800	16,800	
Yale	81,746	44,448	37,298
27 University Library Total	$1,080,522	$687,378	$393,144

Plus Library of Congress ($141,502 + $14,817 = $156,319)
Grand Total **$1,236,841**

a. 1977-78 figures   b. 1978-79 figures

173

APPENDIX IV:
Geographical Distribution and Subject Matter

East (10 Libraries)	Cataloged Volumes	Number of Titles by Subject (Law, Fine Arts, Special Collections excluded)						
		General	Phil/Rel	Hist.	Lang/Lit	Soc.Sci.	Other	Total
Harvard-Yenching	154,183	5,318	12,183	19,610	20,760	20,692+	7,659	86,222
Yale	113,044	2,059	3,709	17,247	12,119	10,155	4,378	49,667
Columbia	113,597	4,757	5,542	18,743	13,693	16,560	5,680	64,975
Cornell	32,900	795	500	2,156	3,070	1,536	897	8,954
Rochester	10,894	201	371	1,371	1,844	600	486	4,873
Princeton	70,774	1,622	3,016	8,437	7,926	7,081	1,689	29,771
Pennsylvania	23,400	333	790	1,851	2,988	863	394	7,219
Library of Congress	260,000	7,219	11,864	33,595	38,270	68,870	35,668	195,486
Maryland	27,787	509	1,551	5,276	7,637	4,158	1,706	20,837
Pittsburgh	12,138	145	315	1,831	844	994	172	4,301
East Totals	818,717	22,958	39,841	110,117	109,151	131,509	58,729	**472,305**
Midwest, Texas (10 Libraries)								
Ohio State	10,971	91	105	705	1,870	405	166	3,342
Michigan	144,088	3,008	2,905	16,100	13,190	13,518	4,771	53,492
Indiana	23,290	554	765	2,479	3,388	1,068	703	8,957
Wisconsin	31,471	310	1,340	5,610	7,613	1,625	862	17,360
Minnesota	18,090	128	340	1,647	2,847	1,054	184	6,200
Chicago	89,485	2,722	4,321	10,706	11,725	9,988	2,993	42,455
Illinois	32,000	716	1,096	3,890	4,611	3,781	1,156	15,250

(10 Libraries)	Cataloged Volumes	Number of Titles by Subject (Law, Fine Arts, Special Collections excluded)						
Midwest, cont.		General	Phil/Rel	Hist.	Lang/Lit	Soc.Sci.	Other	Total
Washington Univ.	41,809	769	1,093	3,258	4,570	2,283	1,242	13,215
Kansas	19,000	209	238	1,609	1,312	1,886	572	5,826
Texas	26,994	230	397	2,053	2,452	1,600	219	7,085
Midwest Totals	437,198	8,737	12,600	48,057	53,578	37,208	12,868	173,182
Southwest, Pacific, Northwest (7 Libraries)								
Arizona	23,125	211	634	1,815	2,035	1,440	657	7,675
UCLA	64,000	846	2,019	3,872	4,085	3,169	1,362	15,353
UC-Santa Barbara	21,511	583	585	1,818	1,883	1,558	67	6,494
Hoover	93,611	1,507	2,710	11,230	8,297	25,933	4,017	53,694
UC-Berkeley	146,873	3,395	4,733	12,178	12,693	15,840	5,731	54,570
Oregon	15,400	240	737	1,681	1,584	614	496	5,352
Univ. of Washington	55,700	1,268	1,546	5,436	5,673	4,364	2,113	20,400
Totals	420,220	8,050	12,964	38,030	36,250	52,910	14,443	163,538
Hawaii	66,381	839	2,845	6,383	6,603	5,495	956	23,121
GRAND TOTAL of titles in 28 libraries:								850,328

APPENDIX V:
General Status of Libraries by Size (1979-80)

Library	Programs: faculty enrollment	Holdings: volumes titles	Acquisitions: monographs serials	Book Budget: monographs	Personnel: total salary number of staff
Library of Congress		606,816v. 195,486t.	14,081v. 1,274v. 112 microfilm reels	$141,502 periodicals paid by the serials department	Tokyo office: $123,519 7.5 staff L.C. office: $774,860 36 staff
L.C. Law Library		60,000v. 18,036t.		$14,817	$63,911 3 staff
L.C. Total		666,816v.		$156,319	$962,290

Group I (Over 60,000 volumes)

Library	Programs: faculty enrollment	Holdings: volumes titles	Acquisitions: monographs serials	Book Budget: monographs serials outside	Total	Personnel: total salary number of staff
UC-Berkeley	28 1,512 EA	189,575v. 54,570t.	4,138v.[a] 1,204v.[a] (bound)	$23,770 $34,576 $36,756	$95,102	$115,000 (est.) 4.75 staff and 5 others
Harvard	27	154,368v. 86,222t.	4,088v.[a,b]	$79,311	$79,311	$68,687 5.36 staff and students

Library	Programs: faculty enrollment	Holdings: volumes titles	Acquisitions: monographs serials	Book Budget: monographs serials outside	Total	Personnel: total salary number of staff
Harvard Law		+13,000v. 7,482t.				
Fogg Art Museum		+5,000v. (4,000t.)				
Michigan	22 2,183 EA	148,838v. 53,492t.	4,625v.[a] 653t.	$50,000[b] $52,000	$102,500	$91,596 5.5 staff and 1.5 student
Law Library		+9,300v.				
Columbia	26 310 Japan	156,693v.[b] 64,975t.	3,693v.[a] 16t.	$59,915[a,b] $21,598	$81,513[a]	$80,000 5 staff
Yale	16 105 grads, Japan	119,232v. 49,667t.	3,039v. 1,099v.	$44,448[b] $37,298	$81,746	$117,172 8.5 staff and .6 student
Hoover	25 1,215 EA	101,598v.[a] 53,694t.	2,520v.[a] 290t.	$57,781[b] $5,000	$62,681	$111,070 7.5 staff and .75 student
Washington— Seattle	19 1,409 EA	59,700v.[a] 20,400t.	1,539v.[c] 630t.[c]	$8,508 $20,000 $26,120	$67,778[a]	$62,430 4.1 staff and 2 others
Law Library	4	+30,000v.		$13,150		

Library	Programs: faculty enrollment	Holdings: volumes titles	Acquisitions: monographs serials	Book Budget: monographs serials outside	Total	Personnel: total salary number of staff
Chicago	19 756 EA	89,485v. 42,455t.	3,584v.[a,b]	$7,932 $11,333 $38,860	$58,125	$77,527 5.75 staff and .4 student
Hawaii	87	78,793v. 23,121t.	933v.[a,b]	$26,795 $20,240 $2,800	$49,835	$59,731 3.5 staff and .5 student
UCLA	13	71,200v. 15,353t.	2,062v.[d] 138t.	$14,289 $5,500 8,200	$27,989[d]	$23,689 1.5 staff and .3 student
Princeton	11 30 Japan	70,774v. 29,771t.	3,112v.[a,b]	$34,750[b] $41,210	$75,960	$82,805 5.93 staff and 4.805 student
Total		**1,297,556v.**	**33,333v.**		**$782,640**	**$889,707**
Group II (Over 20,000 volumes)						
Maryland	7 3 PhD cands. Japan	52,787v. 20,837t.		$10,864 $8,155	$19,019	$83,308 4.7 staff and 3.5 others
Washington— St. Louis	8 40 EA	41,876v. 13,215t.	540v. 146v.	$4,500 $6,000 $8,000	$18,500	$22,570 1.5 staff and 2.8 student

Library	Programs: faculty enrollment	Holdings: volumes titles	Acquisitions: monographs serials	Book Budget: monographs serials outside	Total	Personnel: total salary number of staff
Illinois	13 391 EA	35,000v. 15,250t.	1,331v. 356t.	$20,000 $12,000 $10,000	**$42,000**	$40,000 3 staff and .75 student
Cornell	7 219 EA	32,900v. 15,654t.	1,517v.[d]	$13,934 $8,464 $7,000	**$29,398**	$26,500 EA 2 staff and $4,000 student
Wisconsin	9	31,671v. 17,360t.	2,516v.[d]	$12,000 $4,800	**$16,800**	
Kansas	10	29,000v. 5,826t.	1,310v.[a] 225 items	$14,987 $4,800	**$18,987**[a]	$16,000 1 staff, .5 student
Texas	7	28,994v. 7,085t.	956v.[d] 146 items	$10,000 $4,307	**$14,307**[a]	$20,250 1.5 staff, .25 student
Pennsylvania	5 131 EA	25,000v. 7,219t.	90v.[a]	$10,000 $3,000	**$13,000**	$20,000 2 staff
Indiana	9	24,288v. 8,857t.	556v.[a] 107t.[a]	$7,342 $2,800 $12,000	**$22,142**	$13,500[a] .5 staff and . student
Arizona	6 33 Japan	23,125v. 7,675		$20,000 $6,200 $5,000	**$31,200**	$38,002 2.5 staff and .25 student

179

Library	Programs: faculty enrollment	Holdings: volumes titles	Acquisitions: monographs serials	Book Budget: monographs serials outside		Total	Personnel: total salary number of staff
UC–Santa Barbara	5	22,115v. 6,494t.	1,400v.[d] 342t.		$18,000[b]	$18,000	$62,000 EA 3 staff, .6 student
Total		**346,756v.**	**10,216v.**			**$243,353**	**$342,930** 1 EA, 1 not given
Group III (Over 10,000 volumes)							
Minnesota	9 12 Japan	18,290v. 6,200t.	540v. 120t.	$9,380 $3,000		**$12,380**	$69,000 EA 3 staff, 1.5 Japanese
Oregon	6	15,364v. 5,241t.	945v.[d] 118 items	$6,350 $5,320	$1,500	**$13,170**	$11,660 .6 staff and .25 student
Pittsburgh	6	13,000v. 4,951t.	930v.[d] 280 items	$11,903 $4,434		**$16,337**	$22,060 1.58 staff and .5 student
Ohio State	8 692 EA[d]	12,476v. 3,362t.	650v.[d] 62 items	$8,235 $1,907		**$10,142**	$26,836 2 staff and .25 student
Rochester	5	10,894v. 4,873t.	202v.[a] 113 items	$1,500 EA $2,500		**$2,500**	1 staff (EA) and 1 student
Totals		**70,294v.**	**3,267v.**			**$54,529**	**$129,556 (EA)**

a. 1978–79   b. figure includes serials   c. 7/78 –2/79   d. 1977–78

APPENDIX VI:
Library Holdings in Selected Topics (Number of Titles)

	Buddhism	Local History	Manyōshū	Genji Monogatari	Bashō	Saikaku	Natsume Sōseki	Mori Ōgai	Akutagawa	Dazai Osamu	Mishima Yukio	Kawabata Yasunari
Berkeley	1943	2807	280	200	140	50	85	50	40	60	45	40
UCLA	1324	515	125	103	50		27		56	58	50	47
Chicago	1890	1125	215	175	146	90	145	16	24	48	25	27
Columbia	2598	3332	275	149	143	100	65	85	75	80	100	75
Harvard	5993	3822	370	240	190		180					
Hawaii	1701	1294										
Hoover	323	1130	115	130	65	67	50	20	15	30	30	20
Illinois	309	289	40	45	55		50					
Lib. of Congress	4275	3165	210	150	150	80	80	45	50	75	95	50
Maryland (mostly pre-1950 imprints)		259	65	50	100		95			55	14	45
Michigan	1355	4075	275	224	175	80	105	55		60	68	52
Princeton	1374	1137	195	125	108		90	45		45	30	35
Yale	1375	1991	250	225	150	125	140	70	75	50	150	75
Wisconsin	495			170								
Minnesota			255									
Washington—Seattle	1110	1120	156	122	65	100	121	70	58	49	105	75

MICHIGAN PAPERS IN JAPANESE STUDIES

No. 1. Political Leadership in Contemporary Japan, edited by Terry MacDougall.

No. 2. Politics, Candidates, and Voters in Japan: Six Quantitative Studies, edited by John Creighton Campbell.

No. 3. The Japanese Automotive Industry: Model and Challenge for the Future?, edited by Robert E. Cole.

No. 4. Survey of Japanese Collections in the United States, 1979-1980, by Naomi Fukuda.